EMOTIONAL BUSINESS

EMOTIONAL BUSINESS

Inspiring Human Connectedness to
Grow Earnings and the Economy

RAVI RAO, MD, PhD, MEd

iUniverse, Inc.
Bloomington

Emotional Business
Inspiring Human Connectedness to Grow
Earnings and the Economy

iUniverse books may be ordered through booksellers or by contacting:

iUniverse
1663 Liberty Drive
Bloomington, IN 47403
www.iuniverse.com
1-800-Authors (1-800-288-4677)

Because of the dynamic nature of the Internet, any web addresses or links contained in this book may have changed since publication and may no longer be valid. The views expressed in this work are solely those of the author and do not necessarily reflect the views of the publisher, and the publisher hereby disclaims any responsibility for them.

Any people depicted in stock imagery provided by Thinkstock are models, and such images are being used for illustrative purposes only.

Certain stock imagery © Thinkstock.

ISBN: 978-1-4759-2617-0 (sc)
ISBN: 978-1-4759-2619-4 (e)
ISBN: 978-1-4759-2618-7 (dj)

Library of Congress Control Number: 2012908411

Printed in the United States of America

iUniverse rev. date: 6/20/2012

For all those who have taught me where
emotion truly resides

Contents

Preface: The Author's Journey

From where does an original business perspective emerge?

For some great ideas, conception occurs amid friends jotting their conversation on a cocktail napkin. Brilliance bursts within an inspired moment of bouncing thoughts back and forth, sometimes sitting in the most ordinary of neighborhood pubs or dormitory rooms. Their words become innovations that change the world.

Other groundbreaking insights are derived not from words, but rather from a rigorous review of facts. Like a meticulous miner of numerals, a dedicated researcher spends many sleepless months trying to extract a conclusion buried deep within a mountain of statistical correlations. The quest may yield a diamond after such labor, but the seeker never knows at the start if the treasure is really there or whether she has embarked on a fruitless expedition.

Eureka and Data are not common names for parents, but their offspring are numerous and impressive.

Emotional Business, however, is born from a different father. My view of companies, and the role of organizations within the broader human condition, is neither a sudden revelation nor the fruits of a research endeavor. Instead, this book is the result of gradually accumulated lessons over the last twenty-five years. The insights within are an amalgamation of what

I have observed through three lenses of *babies, brains,* and *business.*

In the 1980s, my eyes were opened to the pathways of human development. During my collegiate and master's studies in child development, I gained an awareness of the balance between what infants are inherently born with (emotional nature) versus what is acquired by experience (emotional nurture). I was immersed in studying theory but also spent vast hours interacting with children in schools, and as a researcher. To this day, I still find myself watching with amazement the complex behaviors of babies and preschoolers. Throughout this text, I offer examples of infant actions as demonstrations of the biological predisposition of humans to be emotionally responsive to their environments.

The second of my formative experiences came during an intense decade spent in the academic/medical hallways of Johns Hopkins, the University of Virginia, and Harvard. Numerous scholars in neuroscience, neurosurgery, and pediatrics were my tutors of the architecture of the brain. Two doctoral degrees and operative training in pediatric neurosurgery gave me a privileged view inside the skull and an appreciation for the brain as the center of all we consider as human emotion. I continue to philosophically view human existence as a reflection of the brain's inherent structure and capabilities.

Upon leaving the operating room in 2000, I was afforded the chance to enter the corporate world into one of the world's most influential management consulting firms. After several years of conducting financial and strategic assessments, I launched my own solo consulting practice focused on managing improvement programs for multinational companies and creative teams. Many of the business assertions made in the chapters ahead are drawn from my work with organizations on five continents. *I owe the business insights of this book to the tens of thousands of people I've met in client companies over the past decade* who asked me questions of *why* something was happening within their organizations. My eclectic path led me to these conclusions, and I hope others will find the lessons meaningful for them.

My intention in writing this book is to inspire a movement to transform business practices. I hope that readers from both small and large companies will discover techniques that will herald in a new era for business.

As the focus of this book is practical action rather than proof of concept, there are no research findings or data references to support each assertion. Anatomical and biochemical information is presented as widely accepted knowledge to be found in any introductory neuroscience or neuropsychology textbook. The intent of this text is to offer a practical manual for reshaping organizations rather than a treatise of brain physiology or the final report of a journalistic investigation.

The first two chapters of this book explain *why* emotion is relevant in business. Readers will encounter a mix of philosophies, fables, examples, and holistic perspectives along with introductory neuroscience. The remaining nine chapters specifically describe *how* emotion can be applied to grow earnings. I offer frameworks, tactics, and strategic checklists that I've refined over time, working with clients.

My long-term hope is that the effort to bring *Emotional Business* to others, born from the gradual accumulation of diverse experiences, will inspire others to build on what is presented here with additional works born from the alternate ancestries of inspired insight and analytical research.

R.P.R.
Chicago, January 2012

Chapter One:
The One-Handed Civilization

Several millennia ago, in a place now forgotten by the memory of time, an empire existed unlike any other.

On one fateful day, when the mighty ruler had ventured for a walk outside of his palace, a scorpion bit him and caused his right hand to become permanently paralyzed. Despite his distinguished record of bravery and phenomenal intellect, the limitation of his hand movements led him to doubt himself. He worried that his hand would attract more attention than his leadership.

In an effort to appease the insecure nature of their emperor, the clerics and his elite inner circle began to adapt the palace environment for him. Doors were adjusted to utilize left-handed movement. Small tools and eating utensils were reshaped to his convenience.

Still feeling awkward in the company of others, the emperor was pleased when the smaller improvements of the castle architecture were later accompanied by an unspoken rule that all servants, guards, and citizens should use only their left hand when in the company of the emperor. Every individual knew that to risk using both right and left meant offending the ruler and perhaps incur harsh repercussions. One-handed action was the only acceptable action.

It was not long after that the left-handed conventions propagated beyond the walls of the palace into the villages and vast regions of the empire. The mighty emperor served as a model for others in all respects of his life, so the thinking went, and as such his paralysis was interpreted to be either divine intervention or the basis of a new code of conduct for everyone to follow.

The emperor's long life sustained the expectation for one-handed activity over the ensuing decades. Profound changes were seen in both grand and granular aspects of daily living. Cooking, cleaning, tending to animals, caring for children, handshake greetings, and tasks of ordinary existence were done with only the left hand.

Slowly, generations began to internalize the one-handed expectation as accepted code of behavior, and not simply an obligation to follow. Parents scolded young children if they reached for objects with their right hand. Mentors trained their apprentices in left-handed skilled trades. Leaders and intellectuals promoted the inferior nature of the right side. Merchants only offered left-handed products.

Those involved in agriculture and carpentry silently questioned the wisdom of the unilateral restriction on their vocations. Activists pointed to the biological minority of individuals born left-handed as an argument for creating right-handed strategies. Some bold heretics implored, "Surely there must be a better way," but their suggestions were met with disapproval by those elites who preferred the stability of unnatural restrictions to following inherent human tendencies.

The emperor died many decades later, but by then the citizens had forgotten why they had originally switched to the left-only way of living. His demise did not trigger the demise of a cultural norm throughout the empire. The one-handed civilization continued even after his death for other emperors. People had, over time, simply accepted that one entire side of their body was somehow inferior to the other side and lived in accordance with that belief.

The one-handed civilization persisted for many years until the evolving needs of humanity and threats from other empires forced change. Warfare, and then rebuilding after war, required two-handed effort. Out of desperation to survive, people reexamined their historical inclinations. They questioned whether their aspirations would not be better served by using both right and left hands.

The one-handed civilization is a mythical fable invented to illustrate a weighty idea: *an entire culture can be, for a variety of reasons, led to believe something that is neither in its best interests nor aligned with the instincts of the human species.* It may, over time, begin to unquestioningly accept a false premise. The ramifications of such thinking can be profound, pervasively affecting many elements of people's lives. Such blind allegiance to legacy ideas is eventually reexamined only when it is clear that survival is at stake.

Our Own One-Handed Civilization

The premise of *Emotional Business* is that a similar tale can be written about the way humans have constructed companies since the advent of industrialization. In the past two centuries, we have not improperly separated right from left; rather, we have accepted the improper separation of business success from emotional success. While the separation may have served well the needs of business owners and shareholders for multiple generations, blind allegiance to separating emotions from business now threatens the viability of businesses everywhere. Importantly, emotional excellence must be recognized as an addition to the fundamentals of a successful business, not a substitute for what ensures business success today. Business

3

success and emotional success are the separated right and left hands of the modern global economy; we need both to be successful.

The schism between business activities and emotional experience is pervasive in modern times. From the frontline clerk to the CEO, the modern worker (in both Eastern and Western cultures) has been indoctrinated to suppress the human brain's emotional instincts in favor of remaining dispassionate, disengaged, and even disingenuous in order to succeed professionally.

At the executive level, leaders have been conditioned to ignore crucial emotional information—the inadequacies within the customer experience, the flawed emotional dynamics of the management team, the inefficiencies arising from conflicted business units, the relationship wounds from a plant closure or new corporate acquisition, the lack of integrative values within the company—such that metrics solely drive decisions despite the intrinsic incompleteness of data. The unemotional upper echelon is driven by numerical outputs. Ignorance of underlying emotions can lead to catastrophic failure of a new initiative or merger or operational system, but this fact is not always recognized.

Individual leaders also face a false dichotomy to forge their identity as a rigorous, results-oriented tyrant or be a nurturing, naive softy who doesn't meet targets. In some settings, an individual leader is perceived as powerful and effectual only if she is unemotional. Contrary to the expectation that leaders can emulate machines, positions of power are actually centers of intense emotional experience; responsibility, loyalty, and trust are profound concerns in the mind of a leader. Nonetheless, the business climate has favored delegitimizing such emotional considerations. The instinct of a spectacular leader is to have emotional awareness of those around him in order to support the requirements for long-term company success. Today, this leadership instinct is suppressed.

Emotion and business functioning are separated not only within executive ranks, but throughout the employee hierarchy as well. Peers are frequently afraid to socialize (i.e., build collaborative networks) for fear of their manager doubting their productivity. New job candidates are scrutinized for their analytical skills but far less so for their communication skills, even though a lack of teamwork can have severe effects on results.

Many employees are supervised by intense attention to metrics in a way reminiscent of control panels of large machines. Frontline workers spend excessive hours completing time sheets and updates to performance indicator scorecards. When a human deviates from the constancy of a machine, then corrective action is applied.

While measurement provides a certain form of clarity that can support success, there is a point of diminishing returns where too much measurement interferes with results. For example, if a company has twenty-six monthly key performance indicators (KPIs), is the word "key" still necessary? With such hypermeasurement, valuable time is spent on the act of measuring rather than producing.

Minimizing emotions may at first seem like an appropriate business reflex: "Let's just do the work" sounds like a good way to avoid confrontation, disappointment, vulnerability, and frustration. Likely, no single person feels able to address the bigger culture challenges facing the company. Yet over time, this avoidant response fails the organization, as it ignores problematic emotional dynamics until they are too pervasive to fix.

The worlds of humor and entertainment have recognized the ludicrous nature of stoic interactions in business. Comics such as *Dilbert* and television programs such as NBC's *The Office* are beloved because they genuinely reflect the widespread familiarity with uninspiring workplaces.

The minimization of emotion extends beyond the walls of a company to the interface with customers. While companies may boast in glowing terms of their customer service aspirations, the reality is that stressful confrontations occur daily in numerous industries, ranging from airlines to health care. Staff indifference to customer concerns has become so widespread in retail settings that there is little difference between a human-run delivery system and an automated kiosk.

When did this separation of business from emotion begin? A scorpion bite to a mythical emperor's hand suggests that a single event can trigger such an era, but the path to emotionless business was more gradual.

In the 1800s, the Industrial Revolution emphasized the capacity of *machines* as the primary predictor of business output. Individual smiths and tradesmen became less common, while workers in massive factories focused on large-scale production became the norm. The best businesses had the best machines; the idealized unemotional, asocial workers existed only to operate the machines. As machines don't possess emotions, the initial industrial organizational model presumed no emotions to exist within the overall business model.

The Industrial Revolution also altered the emotional interface between buyer and seller. Historical small-scale commerce among artisans, shopkeepers, and buyers was facilitated by long-standing relationships. It was important to know the name of the person who made your shoes or the strawberry jam on the family's dining table. In contrast, industrial commerce between large-scale producers, retailers, and consumers became conducted in an aura of anonymity. No one could possibly know the name of the person who managed the cutter or compressor in the enormous factory that made various household goods. Ultimately, the spread of industrialization became synonymous with depersonalization.

Industrial philosophy thus favored the creation of emotionally disengaged businesses and an economy comprised of emotionally ignored consumers. This philosophy has not been without criticism, however; is it really a coincidence that outcries of the evils of capitalism (including socialism and the contemporary Occupy movement) have come when business has deemphasized emotion? It is easy to mistake the evils of emotionless business as the evils of capitalism.

The emotionally minimized model of business may have worked successfully for an extended era to generate profits, but now, *profound changes are occurring across the globe that will force organizations to revisit the emotionless expectation for leaders and the workforce.*

The most significant of these changes is the evolution of the outputs of business itself. Companies have shifted from goods to services, from mass-designed to customized, from provincial to international. The asocial partitioning of people prompted by the industrial manufacturing approach of two hundred years ago is incongruent with business today. The modern knowledge-based, service-centered, design-enhanced global economy elevates healthy collaboration to a business imperative.

Even the role of people vis-à-vis machines has changed in recent years, prompting a heightened role for emotional sophistication in the manufacturing environment. Once upon a time, the machine was the center of the factory, and the human operated it. Today, with strict regulatory oversight across numerous sectors and a proliferation of product offerings, the primary role of many workers in sites of complex manufacturing and materials processing is to work with other humans.

In production facilities for industries as varied as pharmaceuticals, packaged goods, or petroleum refining, multifunctional teams now ensure quality and functionality of systems. Supervising a production line requires an end-to-end view of numerous subsystems, such as raw materials handling, processing, packaging, and shipping. If the team members do not understand how to listen and resolve conflicts with colleagues of varied backgrounds, production quality suffers as a result.

Collaborative capabilities are readily apparent to customers. Internal asynchronies of a company expose emotional flaws; mishaps in the transfer of information, seamless service, or deflective comments like "You'll have to call another department" trigger backlash and lost loyalty.

Further adding to the changing business landscape are emotionally volatile consumers. With social networking technologies, any celebrity with a complaint is now able to scream his frustration through his electronic megaphone to ten thousand potential customers, who are collectively pulled into the maelstrom of emotional dissatisfaction.

Companies thus find themselves in a messy transition, using an outdated organizational philosophy for a modern economy. Today's business environment requires knowledge sharing, creative innovation in teams, multifunction alignment, and responsive service.

So what will determine success? Emotion.

The historical attempt to exclude emotion from the business environment may ultimately have been a futile and counterproductive objective, no different from trying to avoid the right hand in daily living. Chapter Two explores the emotional nature of the human brain and the provocative concept of *social neuroscience*: The hundred billion neurons within each human brain are responsible for individual thought but also for emotional awareness and connection to others. Our individual brains are part of a broader network of neurons, spread within the species to promote survival through relying on each other for protection, support, and inspiration.

Said differently, even though emotions are an omnipresent attribute of human experience, we have attempted to create emotion-free business environments. This approach is bound to fail given the nature of the emotional brain and the biological predisposition of our species to feel. The Industrial Revolution aspiration for an emotion-free environment can ultimately be achieved only in a human-free environment.

Now is the time to grow individual company earnings and the collective economies of the world by applying insights about the neuro-emotional nature of the human species.

The Three Emotional Hurdles of Commerce

Modern economies have been built on the interdependence of humans to meet each other's needs. The seven billion people on the planet do not survive single-handedly. Each person does not grow his own food on a small swath of land, build his own shelter out of nearby wood, or reach into his own mind for entertainment.

The essence of modern life is that large collections of people are involved in providing increasingly specialized needs to each other. The provision of such (basic and esoteric) needs creates employment and socially rewarding roles for others, who in turn create market demand for additional products and services. Each person survives due to the efforts of thousands of others.

At the foundation of such interdependency is trust, the ability to exhibit personal vulnerability in the belief that another person/party will offer something back that is valuable. In the case of commerce, the buyer trusts that giving money to the seller will be reciprocated with a reliable product or service. Credit and other financial services are based on the assumption that people can be trusted to repay their obligations. Manufacturing is predicated on people trusting each other for layers upon layers of decisions within a supply chain.

Of course, many unscrupulous practices and practitioners exist, and thus every economic system must also implement legal safeguards and regulations to ensure that transactions can continue in an aura of transparency. When a company or an entire industry is found to have conducted business without regard to customers or investors, then the overall system loses the trust of the population.

"Trust" as a word might bring to mind fuzzy philosophical and spiritual connotations, but *trust is a biological state grounded in a low level of the catecholamine hormones activated when we are threatened* (sometimes called fight-or-flight response, discussed more fully in Chapter Two).

Commerce is a neuro-emotional event. When one individual offers a product or service for sale, the brain of a potential buyer begins a threat assessment of that offer. Fear, desire, or emotional connectedness may be experienced. Giving up scarce resources (i.e., currency) raises individual vulnerability, which triggers protective instincts to avoid being disappointed, taken advantage of, and other bombshells. The brain balances the logical elements of the decision with instinctive perceptions of seller trustworthiness.

The model of human interdependency requires overcoming three separate emotional hurdles for commerce to occur:

1. Is it safe to spend? The buyer must believe that the *system itself can be trusted* and will not hurt him now or in the future.
2. Does this item meet my need? The buyer must believe that *the service/product (and its associated buying process) will not leave him disappointed.*
3. Is this the right person/place to buy from? The buyer must believe that the *specific vendor/seller can be trusted* and will not hurt him now or in the future.

The first hurdle speaks to the correlations between emotion and macroeconomics, while the second and third emotional hurdles relate to the application of social neuroscience by an industry or company.

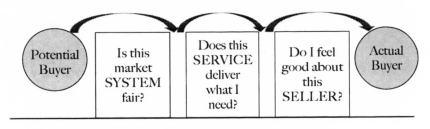

The Three Hurdles of Commerce

Growing an Economy through Emotion

The downturn in the global economy since 2008 and rising fears about long-term government stability have taken attention away from the role of emotion within economics at exactly the time when it has *risen* in importance.

Just as individual companies migrated two centuries ago to an emotionless form of conduct, so too did the collective macroeconomic pattern. Economic growth had previously been driven by the entrepreneurialism of vast numbers of small businesses, each interlinked by personal relationships within cities and communities; a thriving economy indicated a high degree of trust, relationships, and emotional connectedness between buyers and sellers. Each was willing to invest in each other to improve overall quality of life. A flourishing economy reflected an emotionally connected citizenry.

As the depersonalization effects associated with industrialization became widespread, economic growth occurred without an assumption of emotional connectedness between buyers and sellers. Instead, people were assumed to make buying decisions entirely out of individualistic interest.

In modern times, gross domestic product and other measures of prosperity are characterized as the result of nonemotional factors, such as changes in interest rates, capital availability, taxation, and infrastructure investments. However, experience with manipulation of such factors by governments

11

and central banks has not always led to intended effects; it just isn't that easy or predictable.

The missing consideration in such macroeconomic analyses and interventions may be the *emotional state of the population* involved. If the three emotional hurdles involved in commerce (trust in system, trust in services, trust in seller) are not simultaneously addressed, then government and central bank efforts may be of limited benefit.

For growth to occur, citizens need to fundamentally believe that the broader system itself does not pose a threat to them; this basic expectation was shaken in recent years given the simultaneous collapse of financial services, manufacturing, and real estate in the United States and Europe. Workers and investors at all levels of the wealth spectrum questioned the permanence of institutions with distrust not seen since the Great Depression of the 1930s.

Even with the array of financial interventions that governments made, recovery across the globe was sluggish, in part because of insufficient emotional interventions. Government bailouts of particular industries may prevent imminent collapse, and cash infusions can deflect systemic risk, but they only help an economy to recover if they restore emotional trust in the broader system. Individuals still felt wary of buying, and companies held on to cash reserves rather than making new investments or new hiring.

When such an emotional cloud hangs over a nation, a president or prime minister may do more for the economy by reassuring the frightened populace than any other specific measure. Declaring a clear short-term road map as well as offering an inspired vision of the future can minimize worry and restore confidence (see Chapter Eight for further description of the emotional role of leaders). Specific plans with specific strategies provide reassurance; a program of diagnostic assessments and "stress tests" doesn't inform people about what to expect next. Tangible investment projects and distributions of capital allow people to feel that restoration is occurring, but must be supported by public communications of reassurance. Acknowledgment by leaders of a nation's suffering and hardship triggers a sense of common resolve to correct difficult circumstances. Changing the emotional dynamic of a nation may increase aggregate demand that would otherwise not occur; people and groups spend when they believe the future is hopeful. An economic stimulus only works if it is also a stimulus of trust.

The links between emotional ethos of the population and broader economic patterns can go in both positive and negative directions.

In the pattern of optimism, a good economy promotes a sense of trustworthy interconnectedness. People feel positive about the future and view purchases and investments more favorably. They have greater willingness to trust sellers. Once people feel safe, they buy products and build businesses. (Some might argue an alternate explanation that investment perceptions relate more to risk tolerance than emotional trust, but are they actually separate things?) Hopefulness and community bonds within a nation create the sense of interconnectedness necessary to support commerce.

In contrast, when people are scared, they reflexively hold on to resources for self-protection. If uncertainty and fear become chronic conditions, people may begin to doubt the safety of the marketplace and distrust sellers within the marketplace. They are less likely to make purchases and investments, which further worsens the economy through decreased demand. Unfortunately this becomes a self-defeating loop. As trust and hopefulness become entirely absent, commerce does also.

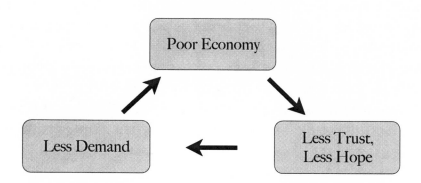

Doom Loop of Economy and Emotion

Judiciousness must nonetheless be applied to interpreting the correlation between emotional health of the population and economic health. Just as a psychiatrically manic individual is not actually in a healthy state of happiness, an economy characterized by unfounded expansion is often in a delusionary state. When a bubble bursts, the fall will be a painful crash. Just as a depressed individual believes things are threats even when objective evidence is to the contrary, a sluggish recovery can be an indicator of a depressed populace. An individual in a healthy emotional state avoids big swings in either direction, and so too does the emotionally healthy economy. Irrational exuberance over market niches creates bubbles; in contrast, healthy emotional connectedness among a population creates sustained economic prosperity.

Earnings in the Era of Emotional Business

Discussion of emotional excellence may seem out of place in a recessionary milieu, where companies are in the midst of downsizing and restructuring. Even though executives may be acutely worried most about cost control, IT, and supply chains, the primary factor that threatens their short-term performance and long-term survival is the ability to embed an emotional strategy for the company.

There is a financial imperative to strategically address fear and uncertainty within an enterprise. Fear leads to withholding key information. Fear leads to overstocking resources and inventory for just-in-case disasters. Fear leads to paranoia or jealousy about colleagues and their intentions. Uncertainty leads to destructive perfectionism and micromanagement. Uncertainty leads to decision hesitation. We chase unreal enemies, we demonize regulators or customers as the source of our problems, and we punish our own people for being human. However, fear is not our only binding emotion within a group. So is connectedness. So is joy. Respect. Purpose.

A new view, that *emotional success and business success are two manifestations of the same underlying human tendencies*, is an argument to bring together two elements that have been historically kept apart. From this perspective, business success actually is dependent on the healthy emotions of leaders, staff, and customers.

The mention of emotions in the workplace may trigger negative connotations, among them irrationality, groupthink, volatility, and distraction. None of these is desirable in the workplace. It is proper and logical to separate business from irrationality and other ills. Nonetheless, it is a mistake in the opposite extreme to remove all emotional awareness from a business enterprise.

For those business leaders who worry that such reunification would create work environments in which they would feel uncomfortable or out of place (e.g., excessive hugging, touching, or crying), such is not the case. Rather, emotion should be thought of in similar ways to IT, supply chain, or finance: an attribute for which a company must be clear about the range of options available and for which a clear strategy must be developed. We would mock a corporation that says, "We avoid IT because it is messy," but we accept such assertions about emotion.

Rather than simply an amorphous concept or a holistic philosophy for business leaders to concur with, emotional success within a business requires particular operational practices and duties of organizational leadership. For an individual company, overcoming the second and third emotional hurdles to commerce (i.e., trust in product and trust in seller) requires specific tactics along four emotional interfaces:

1. The customer experience
2. The team experience
3. Internal stakeholders resolving their conflicts
4. Connectedness among coworkers as the foundation of an "emotional strategy" for a business

Improving these interfaces requires a combination of investments in process redesign, training, internal communications, organizational development, and corporate priorities. As a helpful supplement to the upcoming chapters, the Appendix of this text contains outlined lists of each set of tactics across the four interfaces.

For the most successful organizations, growing top-line revenues will be a function of understanding the customer experience as an emotional event. Market research will go beyond demand for certain product features, to include demand for certain emotional experiences. For example, it will be relevant for a property insurer to determine that "77 percent of our customers value the empathy of the claims adjuster more than any other factor." Such data influence recruiting, the appropriate metrics of employee performance, and specific marketing campaigns. Chapter Three reviews the seven emotional needs of customers.

For the most successful organizations, success will come from reaping the rewards of multifunctional teams who can integrate diverse ideas into exemplary insights, products, and outcomes. Emotional awareness will be a hallmark of team processes and leadership development. Chapter Four reviews the nine emotions within successful teams.

For the most successful organizations, departments and business units will learn to coexist on the same page, using a common vision and alignment. Chapter Five reviews ways to identify if internal conflict is depleting earnings from an organization, along with seven mechanisms to resolve long-standing rivalries and frictions.

For the most successful organizations, an emotional strategy promoting internal connectedness will be the secret that allows them to outperform competitors in their industry. Major strategic decisions, such as acquisitions, degree of leverage, and product pipeline, will be on equal footing with developing a *competitive emotional advantage* for the company. A direct acknowledgment of emotion and its central role in brand, customer experience, employee productivity, and leadership practices will form the basis of superlative market share and market capitalization. Chapter Six describes the nine major emotional strategies for successful companies.

The most successful organizations will also understand how to recover from especially difficult periods. Chapter Seven describes the three patterns of an unsustainable drain on emotional reserves and how companies can recover from painful emotional scenarios.

Leaders within the most successful organizations will understand the application of social neuroscience in how they gather people together, inspirationally communicate, and listen. These capabilities will be a critical part of strategic alignment and earnings generation. Chapters Eight and Nine review these skills in detail.

The most successful organizations will make emotional excellence a clear priority by openly acknowledging the presence of emotional stress within the organization. Chapter Ten describes the myriad of ways that individuals cope with the stress of daily business activities.

The era of emotionally minimized business operations—predicated primarily around machinelike management of humans—is over.

The consequences of poor emotional functioning now include disgruntled buyers, missed sales handoffs, sluggish research and development (R&D) adaptations to the market, stalled decision making, and loss of premier talent. Whether in the interface with customers, the linkages between employees, or the resolution of conflicts within an organization, problems in managing emotions inevitably lead to problems in managing business results.

In other words, if you get the emotions right, you get the business right.

* * *

How Now

The end of each chapter will highlight a short list of immediate tactics that can put the principles described into place within companies, some already mentioned and others that are first described in these lists.

- *Integrate emotional strategy into business planning.* Venture capital funds and angel investors should expect start-ups to develop an emotional strategy document to accurately assess risk. CEOs should state an emotional vision for their companies. Executive teams and consultants should assess goodness of fit among emotional strategies in due-diligence explorations of potential merger-acquisition opportunities (more on this in Chapter Six).

- *Leaders should give a vision address.* Whenever interventions attempt to stimulate economic growth, leaders should supplement such actions with an address to stimulate emotional trust in systems (emotion hurdle 1). Describe how things will look in the future to inspire confidence. Where business leaders have the ear of political leaders, emphasize the need for emotional reassurance as part of a pro-business agenda (more on this in Chapter Eight).

Chapter Two:
Descartes Was Wrong

This chapter describes how emotion is rooted in social neuroscience.

To understand the critical role of emotion in business, one must first understand the critical role of emotion in human survival.

One of the exceptionally consistent foundations of life across every corner of our planet is the strength of groups. Catastrophic forces that would presumably extinguish an individual organism fail to eliminate a group. Solar variations, scarce resources, predator attacks, and numerous unforeseeable threats evoke herd responses of protection. Resilience to unexpected adversity appears as the hallmark feature of successful existence, especially resilience formed via connection to others. Wherever one looks in the jungles, sky, or water, life persists as a result of congregating.

It is no different with humans. Despite the great significance of individuality, it would be a mistake to describe humanity as a disengaged set of seven billion independent entities, each person moving in a solitary path with no mindfulness or connectedness to others. Quite the opposite: humans define much of their life experience based on the emotions generated by specific relationships (e.g., I'm jealous of my sibling, I adore my boss, I'm inspired by my rabbi).

Birds fly together. Horses run together. Fish swim together. Humans feel together.

Defining Emotion

What is emotion? For some, it is the poetic force that prompts noble heroes to rescue someone from harm. Others see emotion as a weakness, a naive flaw that should ultimately be supplanted by logic. The metaphysical view may see emotion and spirit as linked, through which human experience is rendered.

For understanding its role in business, think of emotion as the *inherent tendency of the human brain to find meaning and connection to others* in response to circumstances. This instinct to look for meaning and connection promotes shared survival of the species. The intricacy of emotional experience is nuanced (and has been explored more by poets and songwriters than by neuroscientists). The brain perceives all intense permutations of sadness, anger, fear, joy, and love; the broad umbrella of emotion incorporates distinctions such as embarrassment versus shame, betrayal versus disappointment, worry versus terror. Each reflects how we perceive meaning and connection to others.

Emotion encompasses both internal experiences as well as externally observable behaviors. We don't see internal experience but we can witness external actions. Internal frustration of a coworker is demonstrated by their external complaining. Internal insecurity of a boss is represented by their external micromanagement of others. Internal feelings of connectedness between a director and junior associate are manifested as mentoring and followership.

While outward acts of weeping, complaining, micromanagement, laughter, or yelling are easily recognizable overt signals of emotional state, others are much more subtle. Such *microbehaviors* (actions that involve relatively small changes in outward appearance or activity) allow humans to display emotions to each other through delicate alterations of the facial muscles, body posture, and voice. Even infants display their emotions quite dramatically through facial expressions and vocalizations. (Chapter Nine reviews these in greater detail.)

Cogito Ergo Sum

"I think, therefore I am," said René Descartes, a seventeenth-century French philosopher and mathematician. His idea that cognition and sentience form the basis of existence has influenced commonplace views of the brain as the "thinking" organ. While it is true that computation and creativity occur within the brain, so do compassion and collaboration. The brain is equally the thinking organ and the organ of emotional experience.

While modern vernacular continues to incorrectly emphasize the "heart" as the source of valor and love, neuroscience continues to uncover the elegance of emotional neurochemistry within the brain. With the advent of the functional magnetic resonance imaging (fMRI) and positron emission tomography (PET) techniques in recent decades, neuroscience is in a groundbreaking era of discovery into how emotional experiences are rooted in the brain.

There is a long-standing myth that "we only use 10 percent of our brains." Not so. The revolutionary insights brought forth by modern research have begun to elucidate the interlinked geography of brain regions that underlie emotional interaction and interpersonal experience. We utilize dozens of different centimeter-sized regions within the three pounds of brain tissue to feel the rich panorama of emotions. Research continues to discover even more linkages among those regions. The updated truth to the myth is, "We use *100 percent* of our brain. Science only knows what 10 percent does." And that percentage is growing.

Emotion is built with a different architecture in the brain compared with other functions. While sensory input and movement control tend to be focused in *one* specific brain area—for example, the occipital lobe for vision, the postcentral gyrus of the parietal lobe for touch, the brainstem for heartbeats and breathing—emotion is linked to a diaspora of neurons across the cerebral landscape. It's everywhere. The emotional range of human experience is vast, and a correspondingly vast number of brain areas are involved.

The list of brain locations involved in emotion continues to grow as our understanding of the brain progresses. The regions involved include the amygdala (in the deep section of the temporal lobe), the orbitofrontal cortex (just behind the eyebrows), and the cingulate gyrus (toward the middle of the brain). Mirror neurons are small structures present in multiple locations that allow us to relate to the actions and physical experiences of others. Oxytocin, the substance that promotes intense attachment, emanates from the posterior pituitary. Some of the neurotransmitters involved in emotional states include serotonin and dopamine. In ten years this list will look different, as research continues into how the brain processes various experiences.

Why are so many locations involved in emotion? It is part of the human survival mechanism: *emotion persists* even when specific sections of the brain may be damaged. For example, a stroke to the speech cortex may leave one unable to form words; a blow to the back of the head may cause injury to the visual cortex that leaves one blind. Both of these deficits are tragic but do not necessarily imply death to the individual (or the species) because of the retained ability of the person to form emotional connections. Emotional connection allows the disabled person to remain connected to friends, family, and service providers who help him or her.

The plethora of emotional brain locations has contributed to the survival of the species—the distribution of emotion centers makes it difficult to completely knock out emotion from the brain. Since humans have such a strong inclination to experience emotional connectedness and empathy, the species has survived catastrophic threats by group resilience. The human tendency to coexist as couples, families, villages, and societies most obviously demonstrates this.

Again, one may ask why emotion is so pervasively hardwired within the brain. Why is it an asset to feel connectedness? Emotion is, simply, what allows our species to survive. Our brain's desire and intrinsic tendency to communicate is our greatest evolutionary trait. Other animal species possess flight, better strength, faster speed, crisper vision, superlative smell, and extraordinary hearing. While problem-solving intelligence might be an additional defining attribute of distinction for our species, an individual genius human remains quite vulnerable to other creatures with so many areas of greater ability. It is the capacity of each human to sophisticatedly organize with other humans that gives our species its strength and sustainability. To paraphrase Charles Darwin, it is survival of the fittest groups, not the fittest individual. Humans are frail alone but are impervious together.

As noted earlier, the brain's architecture promotes this shared survival. We are born with the tendency to be aware of others, and thus the brain prompts many ingrained behaviors of unity. This is partly a function of similar architecture in each brain (we all have an amygdala) but also a function of what that architecture is designed to do (we cannot help but notice others around us).

Humans feel together, and often convert internal commonality into joint response. When tragedy strikes an individual or a group, others come to their aid. This is true for both big events, such as natural disasters when international charities are mobilized, as well as smaller events, such as a death in the family that triggers support from friends and acquaintances. This very honed awareness is a component of the emotional survival mechanism for groups.

The implication of these observations is that humans continue as a species not only because of the ability of the frontal lobe to perform abstraction and complex problem solving in the face of threats, but the ability of the brain's emotional neurons to prompt protection of each other. Neurons may be housed in each person's skull, but their ownership is better labeled "cells of the species," in that they communicate and translate the human condition.

Descartes was wrong. It is not "I think, therefore I am."

We feel, therefore we are.

The Pounder and the Waver

True story. It is an ordinary spring weekend in 2011 in the small Los Angeles, California, suburb of Hermosa Beach. The morning sun is shining warmly as various bicyclists, joggers, and surfers head to the ocean to begin their day. At a beachside breakfast restaurant, various individuals, couples, and families convene to have a nice meal.

At one table sits a young mother with two boys, a four-year-old preschooler and a ten-month-old infant. The younger child sits in a high chair. A few tables over, a gray-haired husband, his wife, and their eight-month-old daughter sit down to begin their meals. The young one also has a high chair from which to view her parents and other restaurant patrons. The families don't know each other; they've never met. But from their spots eight feet apart, the two infants make immediate eye contact, as if they are old friends. One smiles, and the other begins to wave her arms.

While the adults and the older sibling are otherwise engrossed in the menu and conversation, the baby girl clasps and unclasps her diminutive fingers repeatedly while looking at the other infant. It is a primitive wave. The second infant smiles brightly in return and begins to smack the table in excitement.

The sound of his small hand striking the varnished wood is barely noticeable; it is neither disruptive nor remarkable in the cacophony of silverware, conversation, and kitchen sounds present in the diner. Nonetheless, the rat-a-tat-tat pounding catches the attention of the other infant, who smiles and waves even more vigorously in return.

The Pounder and the Waver have instituted their own emotional interaction without formalized rules or conventions; they simply express their enjoyment from the acknowledgment of the other. These two children are strangers. Yet, they engage in this back-and-forth emotional tennis for the entire length of their meals with their families, as if they planned to meet each other at the restaurant. They continue to make eye contact for a few more minutes, until her gray-haired father upon departure carries the Waver away.

This simple story of the Pounder and the Waver speaks to the inborn instinct of humans to emotionally connect. We can observe the neurological predisposition of humans to be exceptionally aware of (and influenced by) the emotional signals of others during our earliest days: infants display our species' nature unadulterated by the influence of experience.

Behavioral research with infants over the past century has dispelled the notion that we are born as a blank slate upon which experience is written. Psychologists and pediatricians have studied the very young through structured experiments using videos, interactions with parents, puzzles, and other tests of cognition and emotional capacities. Rather than a blank slate, we are born with innate capabilities to emotionally interact, connect, and comprehend the signals of our environment. The developing brain may not comprehend sentence structure until much later, but the very young infant can determine when to smile and how to engage another person.

The infant's ability to understand emotional signals explains the basis of human survival. Infants cannot gather their own food or water. They cannot create their own shelter. Compared with numerous other species that walk shortly after birth, the human infant can barely move until the end of a year. One might look at the pervasive vulnerability of the human infant and question how any human survives past the first six months. The only skill that supports the survival of the human infant— the only reason that any of us live into adulthood—is the ability to interpret which individuals can be trusted to protect them and which ones cannot. Stated differently, the primary ability of the infant is to *give and receive love*. Babies generate the desire to protect, and they smile and play to solidify the shared emotional bond.

The Pounder and the Waver already are forming protective bonds in their interactions. Such invitations remain true of toddlers and preschoolers as well, who naturally engage others in public places. Emotion appears so critical to early development that infant social interaction and toddler gregariousness are seen in every culture of the world regardless of the degree of industrialization or parenting practices. Humans are inherently interactive and emotionally engaging from a very young age.

But then things change.

Extinguishing the Instinct to Connect

Modern societies are filled with examples where individuals do not possess emotional connectedness; violence, prejudice, persecution, oppression, deprivation, bullying, humiliation, rudeness, absence of etiquette, isolation, and indifference are but a few of the symptoms of a lack of connection.

Where does disconnection begin?

There is an old joke that goes, "You spend the first two years teaching a child to walk and talk. Then you spend the next sixteen years telling him to sit down and shut up." Despite the emotionally interactive nature of the brain, *a child's instincts to connect are unintentionally extinguished by loving adults.*

Children instinctively know when someone needs help; even a toddler in the middle of a tantrum will stop his own tantrum if an infant begins to cry. The toddler midtantrum will point in the direction of the crying infant and say, "Look, Mommy, baby crying."

Yet, it is this helpfulness/awareness reflex that is first challenged by adults. Consider a commonly observed phenomenon in all parts of the world: A two-year old child will instinctively walk toward a crying stranger. As the helpful child approaches the stranger, the parent admonishes the child with shockingly loud exhortations, such as, "Stay away! We don't know him!"

Such parental utterances typically reflect a desire to minimize shame or protect the child from predatory adults; the parents are not malicious in intent. Nonetheless, the combination of the harsh sounds, angry tone, possible physical pain (from a spanking), and associated stress hormone response within the child makes the protective inquiry of a suffering individual far less likely in the future.

In a grocery store, a toddler sitting in a shopping cart will often wave and talk to adults passing by until the parent orders, "Keep your head down and stay quiet until we're home!" Though well-intentioned protectiveness on the part of caregivers may be necessary, the child unfortunately begins to associate his own emotional reflexes with parental punishment.

If every time a child looks at others in a public place he is scolded to "stop staring," then the child will gradually ignore the natural neurological impulse to be aware of others. The child associates approaching someone in a spirit of helpfulness with bringing forth pain from the hand or voice of his parent.

28

The child's brain eventually suppresses the instinct to help in order to avoid future pain.

In a home environment where an emotionally impaired adult cares for an infant, apathy extinguishes that child's instincts to connect. A parent suffering from addiction, clinical depression, social marginalization, unemployment, or a variety of other difficulties is likely to react to a child's enthusiasm with a flat response. The infant/toddler/preschooler will initially brightly smile and seek playful engagement with the distracted adult, only to be ignored repeatedly. In other distressed homes, infants will encounter violence in their attempts at engagement. Finally, the child gives up and sees emotional connection as a futile aspiration.

Loving parents/grandparents may unintentionally contribute to the minimization of emotional instincts by disproportionately training some brain areas while ignoring emotional brain development. Well-intentioned adults will spend a seemingly infinite amount of time teaching numbers, colors, and letters to preschool children but spend almost no time teaching the difference between a sad face and an angry face. They spend even less effort coaching how to respond to disappointment or the hostility of another person. They prioritize reading a book over reading facial emotional signals. If children do not practice emotional recognition and interaction, they will struggle with emotional recognition and interaction.

Children's diminished awareness applies not only to the emotions of others but to themselves as well. Adults train children to conform to expectations rather than emotional honesty. Parents scold young children if they cry and generate punitive responses (e.g., "Don't be a baby") as if emotional expression is an attribute of immaturity. In many cultures, children are taught that it is polite to suppress their true feelings (e.g., "When someone asks you how you are, always say 'fine' regardless of how you feel"). Politeness dictates a socially correct answer rather than an honest expression of suffering or sadness. Over time, these lessons can cause confusion and ultimately shut down self-awareness. It is not uncommon to ask a younger child, "How are you?" to be met with a reply of "I don't know." Many adults are likewise unable to accurately describe their own emotional state, sometimes unaware of the anger or fear or pain they are experiencing.

The traditional school environment emphasizes measures of individual performance from an early age, and unintentionally reinforces the concept of individual fight for survival rather than belonging to the connected group. Preschool and kindergarten children learn important concepts by playing together, but an abrupt transition to didactic lectures and individually isolated desks deprives them of those communal learning opportunities. The nurturing behaviors of hugging and handholding seen commonly in preschool are replaced by bullying a few years later in elementary school. Children who perform well academically may be teased as socially undesirable. Grading performance in early childhood promotes the concept of competition *before* the child has even learned to play with others effectively. Children now sit in many outdoor playgrounds by themselves while playing with electronic devices and smartphones.

In the most affluent and hypercompetitive communities, parents actively discourage studying with other children for fear of losing the competitive advantage. The subtext of this well-intentioned parental and teacher guidance is, "No one is trustworthy as your friend. Never relax or connect. You're always fighting to survive." These messages prime the young child to perceive even the safest suburban school as an emotional war zone; since children face this chronically, they may function in a hypervigilant state from a young age. Children in urban poverty face chronic emotional pressure associated with overwhelming street violence, locking them in to the belief that their entire existence is a fight with others.

These influences, in both affluence and poverty, result in disengaged children all over the world. Eventually, neural pathways become dormant from these repeated signals to minimize emotion. Children become less aware of and less compassionate toward others because they are never encouraged to be aware and compassionate. They have diminished empathy and a diminished sense of duty to others. The instinct to protect and nurture fellow humans is suppressed. Trust is difficult to give or to earn.

Obviously, this doesn't end in childhood. Adults are disconnected from others as well. The crushing influence of a lifetime of broken promises and unfair surprises further disconnects us. Abrasiveness is present in numerous public places and social settings (to which the proponents of more civility will attest).

Emotional Disruption and Commerce

Business faces an uphill challenge. Since society continues to create adults disrupted in their ability to emotionally connect, *the rising importance of emotional excellence in business comes at a historical period when such skills are increasingly scarce.* Exactly when emotional sophistication is most needed, it may be most lacking.

For the individual business manager or executive who leads a group of people, this comes as no surprise. One of the typical surprises for a newly promoted supervisor is the proportion of their time spent on feelings and addressing which employees feel undervalued, neglected, disgruntled, unchallenged, disrespected, and so on. An employee's emotional resilience has been undermined over long developmental periods of childhood and adolescence, but it typically falls to the business manager to address it. To lay such burdensome responsibility on each individual supervisor is unsustainable, particularly in a global economy where emotional success is a prerequisite to business success.

Expecting emotional awareness as a matter of common sense is a perilous path to unmet business goals. The only approach that will work must be an *organizational* emotional strategy. Leaders must come to view their companies as a series of neuro-emotional forces in flux. Just as companies spend huge resources for equipment maintenance, there must be an equal recognition of the need for emotional maintenance. This will be discussed in depth in upcoming chapters.

* * *

How Now

- *Companies teach emotional awareness skills.* Beginning with the executive team and working throughout all layers of the organization, require a training program that focuses on emotional awareness: reading nonverbal emotional signals, listening to customers, and listening to colleagues. Of course, fairly little of such expenditure is popular during periods of restrained spending. That must change (more on this in Chapters Six, Eight, and Nine).

- *Business schools teach emotional awareness skills.* Schools at all levels, but particularly those offering MBA degrees, can make emotional awareness a component of the curriculum. As emotional excellence will increasingly form a component of the leadership tool kit, leaders must learn to lead with acumen in financial dynamics as well as acumen in emotional dynamics.

How Now (for results much later)

- *Grandparents and parents teach emotional awareness skills.* Sitting with a young child or grandchild, an adult can practice making facial expressions of different emotions, even making it fun, such as charades-like guessing game. In a public setting, stand close by and allow children to say hello to other children with other parents. Ask children probing questions about their own emotional state, and teach new adjectives to facilitate emotional understanding. Today's children will run tomorrow's businesses.

Chapter Three:
RSTUVWX

The first of the four emotional interfaces of emotional business is the customer experience. This chapter specifically reviews the seven emotional needs of customers and offers tactics for businesses to successfully deliver those seven emotional customer needs.

Product features and pricing are not the only factors that drive customer behavior. Demand is also shaped by the emotions associated with brands or retail-buying environments. A business may have the lowest prices in the industry but lose out to competitors who are better able to create the desired *emotional experience for buyers.*

As discussed in Chapter Two, humans find connectedness through emotional responses rooted in the brain. Seven emotions enable us to overcome commerce hurdles 2 and 3 (trust in product/service, trust in seller): *protection, loyalty, relationship warmth, freedom, instant fulfillment, amazement, or abundance.* Every customer encounter is a chance for a business to grow its "emotional tribe" created by a combination of these seven connection mechanisms.

The "customer experience" is a collection of emotions encountered during the buying process that foster or inhibit trust. As customers assemble in a retail arena or buyers enter a conference room to negotiate terms and conditions of a major deal, trillions of neurons are assessing threats and seeking signals of trust. There is a vibrant biological dance of electrical signals and hormonal emissions among members of the species to understand what is safe versus a threat.

Grand Opening

Imagine the grand opening of a new store.

Freshly shipped products have been stocked, inventory has been precisely managed, enthusiastic workers have been hired, and targeted marketing has been conducted to draw new shoppers in for the first time. Colorful banners inside and outside the building express welcoming greetings.

Executives and frontline clerks are optimistic as crowds gather outside the store before opening, a victorious result of the aggressive advertising launch campaign.

Hundreds of customers walk in during the first few hours. Once within the store, though, things begin to shift for the worse. At an almost imperceptible level, customers experience different forms of emotional disappointment.

An educated customer pulls out five pages of notes he has brought into the store. He seeks out expert help with details of product compatibility, only to be met by mild irritation of a staff member.

A young entrepreneur asks if there is a frequent buyer's rewards program, only to be let down.

A single mother with a crying young child feels embarrassed by icy stares from two staff members; she leaves quickly.

A selective seeker peruses the store offerings but cannot find something that blends all his particular product criteria.

A hurried man buying a single expensive item leaves without making his purchase when he sees the long checkout line.

An affluent buyer peruses aisle after aisle but does not seem to be energized by the items available. As he leaves the store, he calls his friend to share his tragic initial review. "They've got a lot of stuff, but nothing special."

A coupon collector finds no bulk bargains available and becomes disenchanted. She buys only a few small items.

And within a few weeks, the store is practically empty of customers.

The Seven Emotional Needs of Customers

When a business fails to serve the seven emotional customer segments—and therefore fails to create adequate trust—it fails to create the interface that retains customers and grows. The example of the store's grand opening described the implications of failing across multiple emotional dimensions and the resulting financial failure of the business as a result.

As noted earlier, customers are drawn to conditions that promote trust: protection, loyalty, warmth, freedom, instant fulfillment, amazement, or abundance. As this list can be difficult to remember, they can be alternately summarized by the mnemonic sequence RSTUVWX:

R = Responsiveness: "If I have a problem or question, it gets resolved. They've got my back. They're looking out for me."

S = Special status: "I get special treatment because of my loyalty. I'm in the elite program."

T = Tender loving care. "I get treated with kindness. They even remember my name."

U = Uniqueness: "I get it exactly the way I want, with the freedom to choose, customized to my preferences."

V = Velocity: "I get it fast and rarely have to wait."

W = Wow factor: "This is incredible. I love this product."

X = Extra: "I get huge value for what I pay."

Given their universal applicability, customer emotional experiences occur in a wide variety of sales contexts: a traditional brick-and-mortar store, a shopping mall, a food truck, online, an office conference room, a neighborhood coffee shop, and a social chat over a round of golf.

In the future, successful business enterprises must have greater clarity as to their emotional experience proposition for customers. In parallel, customers will become savvy as to their desired emotional experiences.

Just as prices are shopped for today, eventually emotions may also be shopped for. It may never come to the point of labeling two of the emotional needs with a sticker on the front door of a business ("We are a TLC/Extra store"), but that might make things easier!

An emotional experience must avoid *unfair surprises* and *broken promises* for the customer. Emotion is formed with expectations, and violating those expectations is the root of disenchanted buyers. Frontline staff must offer particular actions, behaviors, and verbal exchanges in a consistent manner to ensure that the expectations are met. In the worst case, irritable or apathetic employees represent a "black hole of emotion" for the customer in which none of the seven can be conveyed effectively.

Importantly, *it is counterproductive for a business to attempt to satisfy all seven of the customer emotions.* Each one requires time and significant resource investment to successfully deliver; no company should attempt to be all things to all people. The customer is not always right, because not every customer is right for your business.

The "correct number" of the seven customer emotional offerings for an individual business is not driven by a financial formula; rather, it is a strategic judgment for company leaders to determine. For some enterprises, the best answer is delivering exceptionally on only one of the seven. Doing more than one might require dilution of attention or resources required to be superlative on a given dimension. Other businesses will require a broader net of four or more to attract sufficient revenue from a diverse customer base.

To avoid diluting brand identity, businesses must make the decision to *not* pursue selected elements. There are trade-offs to consider with an increasing breadth of emotional offerings, such as costs of advanced emotional training for staff or capital investments required for store redesign. Partial or insufficient delivery of one of the seven emotional experiences is likely to be a wasted investment.

All businesses large and small should methodically review each of the seven customer emotions as part of their strategic plans and ask two simple questions for each of the seven to determine whether it should be a priority:

1. Is the customer base associated with a particular emotional segment sufficiently large to establish a foundation for growth and/or provide a sufficient return on our investment?
2. Are we as a company prepared to make the necessary investments of training, technology, architectural change, process redesign, talent management, and leadership attention required to deliver this particular emotional experience?

R = Responsiveness

No product or service is ever perfect. Humans are imperfect, and the outputs of human efforts are similarly imperfect. Every company will provide flawed or defective outputs to customers on occasion.

However, even when a product is not perfect, a customer can still develop an emotional connection. If a company is exceptionally responsive to the customer concern when things aren't perfect, it still maintains trust. If a customer feels protected from an adverse outcome, they trust the seller.

For the company that wants to make responsiveness part of the emotional experience of customers, this involves being *accessible* and providing *status transparency* about the customer's concern.

Accessibility implies providing an easy portal through which an issue can be resolved. Customers must easily understand how to obtain the help required and be pleased by the attentiveness and helpfulness of the employee. They want knowledgeable staff to provide them with simple corrective actions or impressive problem solving. Store customers with a question about product features want to easily identify whom to speak with to get their question addressed in a prompt manner. "Let me take care of that for you" is a succinct phrase to convey responsiveness. In contrast, a store employee who looks bothered by a customer question will diminish trust. For the customer who calls a help line, call center staff that play "hot potato" with a customer (i.e., repeatedly transfer the customer) are not providing accessibility. Telling the large client of a services firm "you'll have to talk to the other department about your question" violates the client expectation of responsiveness.

Status transparency allows customers to know where in the processing stream their order/concern is currently. For example, logistics companies offer online tracking to allow both shipper and receiver to precisely know the geographic location of their packages. Numerous banks now provide online account balance information for customers to monitor whether particular transactions have cleared, rather than requiring a phone call or visiting a branch. A simple automated reply when a question is submitted ("Thank you for your e-mail. You will receive follow-up within forty-eight hours") can allay concerns about whether a message was received and create a positive emotional experience. Even if the process in question requires weeks or months to resolve (e.g., a large insurance claim), customers develop a greater comfort knowing where things stand.

S = Special Status

In many industries, a small percentage of customers account for a disproportionate share of revenue. In airlines, there are the frequent flyers. For a family restaurant, there are the Saturday night regulars. For particular technology brands, there are the loyal zealots who buy every device the company produces (e.g., phone, printer, computer, tablet). Losing just a teaspoon of such customers is equivalent to losing gallons of other customers.

Emotional connectedness is often manifested in the form of customer loyalty. Such connectedness is strengthened by a company's recognition of such loyalty as a two-way street.

For the company that chooses to prioritize special status within the customer emotional experience, acknowledging particular customers can be done in five different ways:

1. Price reductions/rebates
2. Upgrades in products/services, faster process
3. Gifts outside of the core business product/service
4. Written and face-to-face expressions of gratitude
5. Special experiences

A large commercial real estate property developer might use special status to build emotional connectedness with tenants by offering, for example: a 10 percent discount for long-time

40

tenants; free warehouse storage space for the largest tenants; thank-you fruit baskets or chocolate boxes; handwritten holiday cards; or invitations sent to the largest tenants to join them in the luxury box suite at the local football stadium.

As you can see by the real estate example, this particular approach to build emotional connectedness with customers requires significant costs and execution planning. Identifying which customers qualify for special status is an operational challenge requiring data tracking (e.g., frequent-flier numbers).

Frontline associates play a crucial role in delivering the special status emotional experience to customers. From a simple verbal acknowledgment ("Thank you for being a Platinum member") to their flexibility in meeting the unique requests of certain customers, this strategy requires an organizational plan of training, incentives, and feedback to consistently deliver.

T = Tender Loving Care

There is an old expression in sales, "People don't care how much you know, until they know how much you care." For certain customers, the need to feel nurtured, supported, and recognized will drive their buying decisions. When such customers feel criticized or disregarded by a company, they take their business elsewhere.

For the customer to perceive tender loving care (TLC) within the buying experience requires going beyond the polite transactional smile. Service firms that are successful at this strategy possess intimate knowledge of the client that goes beyond the facts of his or her account: the client's recent bout with pneumonia, the high school graduation of the youngest child, the customer's pride in the local sports team, or the shared anger over a recent local tragedy.

Additionally, exceptional listening is required within the sales process. (These skills are explored in depth in Chapter

Nine). This must be done in an emotionally authentic manner, such as to not arouse the suspicions of a customer who might perceive disingenuous pleasantries as merely a sales technique. The sales staff must actually care.

TLC has long been the effective emotional strategy of the small-town American diner, where everybody knows everybody. In such locations, "So how's the family?" is a question offered by food servers, long familiar with the life details of the customers. Urban small businesses throughout the world allow customers to linger for hours and be emotionally engaged with other customers and the staff; barbershops, nail salons, coffee shops, pubs, and bakeries are but a few places that support warm friendships.

Tech start-ups and large multinational corporations have also succeeded with this strategy. Buyers of some online sites feel a personal connection to the customer service representatives with whom they speak on the phone. Several large retailers have smiling greeters at the front door of stores to subtly emphasize the interpersonal nature of their sales experience.

Businesses that prioritize the TLC element of the customer emotional experience must hire sales staff, call center personnel, managers, and leaders who emanate approachability and friendliness. Such inherent proclivities can be further refined through formalized training in social neuroscience. Structured feedback mechanisms from customers are also of particular importance in these environments, as they can shape the interactive behavior of the staff on a continual basis.

In this strategy, emotional success with customers requires similar emotional success in interactions among executives, managers, and frontline staff. It is hypocritical to ask staff to care about customers if the company does not also care about the staff. Happy employees will repeat their joyous emotional experience with the customers; emotionally disengaged employees show apathy, resentment, irritability, and anger toward customers.

U = Uniqueness

The joy of choice is an attractive means by which to build emotional connection with customers. The ability to shape the attributes of a product or service is emotionally enticing, as it allows buyers to feel they received it exactly the way they wanted it. One-size-fits-all makes a business much simpler to operate, but offering customers the chance to be "a kid in a candy store" with an array of alternatives is tempting for its revenue potential. Offering such freedom creates trust.

Proliferation of options must be measured against burdens on multiple aspects of the business, including inventory management, supply chain, storage variations, training requirements for production, marketing of a diverse catalog, and organizational structure. The more diverse the catalog of options available, the more difficult is the synchronization of operational elements of the business.

Thus, freedom to uniquely customize can be only an effective emotional experience strategy of a company if there is sufficient operational flexibility in the manufacturing/service process to accommodate adaptations per the customer's need. This is not simple to do.

Consider the simplistic example of a chain of fast-food Italian restaurants. On the menu are calzone options for large versus medium, spicy versus traditional, vegetarian versus meat lovers, sauce inside versus sauce on the side: two-times-two-times-two-times-two requires the operating platform to be able to efficiently produce sixteen different delicious models! Variability makes the product difficult to deliver in a consistent, high-quality manner. Yet, people trust those companies that give them flexibility.

Many businesses have effectively applied the approach of unique customization as part of the customer emotional experience. Systematic fast-food restaurants now include various options for your sandwich, burrito, or combo meal to contain specific vegetables or meats as a result of flexible production systems. Luxury automobiles and high-end computer technology are increasingly sold through advance ordering with specific features. Online purchases of garments now allow the buyer to pick color, size, materials, and other item attributes, where a traditional store might be at zero inventory of the customer's specifically desired item.

Customized insights are also available from service professionals and knowledge workers. Creative designers or management advisers may use a consistent methodology but uniquely package their expertise based on the scope/list of concerns brought by the customer (e.g., freelance consultants craft the depth of their analyses to the customer's wants).

V = Velocity

As Albert Einstein made us realize, all speed is relative. How fast something is moving is always dependent on the speed of the observer. Quantitative measurement of speed does not always correlate with perception. The answer to "Are we moving quickly?" is invariably "Compared with what?"

Pace paradigms for customers have accelerated in the past two decades. Consider the growth of instantaneous activities in multiple cultures around the world: prose e-mails have been replaced by limited-character social networking, and planned gatherings have been replaced by flash mobs and last-minute meet-ups. Corporate bosses expect immediate response to e-mails via smartphones. Customers increasingly expect everything to be instantaneous, even if such expectations are unreasonable.

The emotional experience of speed is related to the brain's chemical reaction to rapid gratification. The subjective perception of waiting promotes physiological fear responses, and fast resolution is pleasurably reinforcing. Process redesign efforts using Lean Six Sigma can be extremely effective at reducing the absolute/objective measurement of waiting times, but such cycle time improvement only has effect on the customer's emotional perception. Again in deference to Einstein, the experience of "Wow, that was fast!" is completely *relative to the emotional expectation* of the customer.

Optimizing the emotional experience of velocity might require trade-offs with other elements of the emotional experience. For example, reassigning staff from the help desk to the checkout line can dramatically improve velocity but will correspondingly reduce the ability to deliver responsiveness. Reducing the number of options in the catalog may significantly increase velocity of service delivery but sacrifices the unique customization component.

Data that provide transparency regarding speed heighten the emotional experience of velocity. *Remind customers how fast the enterprise is.* For example, a highly efficient hospital emergency department might begin to print "your wait time today" at the bottom of the patient's discharge paperwork to emphasize how short the wait was to see a physician (particularly given how slow many competitors are).

W = Wow Factor

From the emotional perspective of the customer, quality is about generating passion for the product/service (i.e., "I love this thing!"). The amazement associated with a "wow factor" provokes a smile, a sense of satisfaction, pleasure, or gratification. The amazement forms trust.

Traditional product quality attributes include criteria such as functionality (i.e., it does what it claims), durability, and an aesthetically pleasing design. Service quality attributes have tended to mix various parameters depending on the industry but often include expertise (e.g., "She really knew her stuff") and accuracy (e.g., "They fixed it right the first time"). These elements remain important and should continue to be emphasized in the design and delivery of products and services.

However, qualitative "wow factors" create an emotional reaction for the customer in several ways:

1. Unexpectedly strong degree of result achieved
2. Unexpected qualitative nature of result achieved
3. Unexpectedly fun delivery mechanism
4. Unanticipated ancillary benefits

The sports car's sensation of dramatic acceleration, the extra storage space in the beautiful house for sale, the captivating aroma of the new pasta sauce, the latest "cool app" for a smartphone, the lifelike resolution of the new plasma screen television, the handwritten welcome note on elegant parchment from the hotel manager, the multimedia deliverables from the consulting firm (when only a paper document was the expectation), the delicate silk used to wrap a gift, the minimal environmental impact of new recycled packaging, the contribution of proceeds to an outstanding charity, and the great taste of the weight-loss food all deliver amazement.

X = Extra

It is one of the most tantalizing words in all of sales: extra. Abundance is an inherently emotionally satisfying experience, in part because much of the history of humanity has been rooted in overcoming the adversity of scarce resources. Customers feel a sense of joy leaving the store if their expectations were surpassed and if they are convinced they were not tricked or ripped off. This is true of low-price, frequent purchase items, such as a gallon of milk, as well as high-price, rare purchase items, such as automobiles.

Customers have a positive emotional experience of extra/abundance if they can say, "I get a huge deal for what I pay."

They must sense that, in their shopping experience, they received *tangible volume* with an *absence of deceit*.

Abundance is demonstrated most directly by *tangible volume*. The growth of stores that routinely sell forty-pound containers of ketchup speaks to the emotional desire for abundance. Other examples include "buy one, get one free" and large portions at a family restaurant. Receiving an impressively large document at the end of a professional services engagement is another form of abundance. All these examples make customers *feel* that their purchase has delivered abundance to them.

Today's customers are wary of things that sound too good to be true. The *absence of deceit* is an emotional need derived from fear. "This sounds like a bargain, but how do I know it isn't a fraud?" runs through the minds of shoppers. To allay this concern, *transparent written comparison* is the most useful manner to demonstrate authenticity. Numerous examples of price transparency exist. Grocery stores and department stores now print a "you saved $X.XX today" statement at the bottom of the sales receipt. Professional service firms don't offer bulk discounts but will offer a "summary statement of achieved progress" to provide written transparency to the client (i.e., emotional reassurance) showing that the client investment has been appropriate and exceptionally productive.

Example #1 of RSTUVWX: Auto Insurance Services

As noted earlier, it is impractical for a company to invest in all seven elements to the degree necessary to create an emotional experience for customers. Sometimes, competitors within an industry will emphasize different elements to gain market share.

As an example, consider how different groups within the auto insurance industry might hypothetically apply the RSTUVWX framework in their operational and marketing/

branding efforts. (The ideas here are fictional and do not reflect actual advertising campaigns of any insurance companies.)

R = Responsiveness: "Sign up for SMS text alerts on your claim, and know right away when your claim has been processed."

S = Status: "Now get rewards points for each auto policy with us, points you can use for free airline flights or hotel stays."

T = TLC: "When Gabriel was injured, his auto insurance agent visited him in the hospital. Does your auto insurance company care enough about you?"

U = Uniqueness: "We've never had anyone ask us for policies to cover a condo, a Chevy, a child, and a Chihuahua. Until today."

V = Velocity: "Order a pizza. Then call us for auto insurance coverage. After you're done, you'll still have a few minutes to wash up before dinner."

W = Wow factor: "Our policy now includes installation of the latest safety alert technology in your car. In the case of a severe collision, a small device in your dashboard will automatically send an alert to the emergency medical services as well as the insurance company to file your claim for you."

X = Extra: "Buy auto coverage, and receive renter's insurance for one year at no additional charge."

Example #2 of RSTUVWX: Academic Medical Center Services

Consider the application of emotional experience to the daily operations of a large urban university medical center. These are hypothetical ideas (not recommendations) and would need to be prioritized, evaluated, and balanced against the broader strategy and regulations of any institution.

R = Responsiveness: A "clinical concierge" on each floor can assist family members with questions or concerns.

S = Status: Near the pediatric intensive care area, there is a residential-style area (with kitchen and laundry room), with special ID access only for families who have children in the hospital for more than thirty nights.

T = TLC: Nurses, physicians, and administrators are trained in the social neuroscience skills of listening and empathy to deliver emotionally exceptional care (see Chapter Nine).

U = Uniqueness: Patients are offered bed/mattress/blanket options, food options, music options, entertainment options, and garment options.

V = Velocity: Streamlined emergency room processes guarantee a wait time of less than sixty minutes.

W = Wow factor: Outbound transportation is provided for inpatients to their home at discharge.

X = Extra: Families of inpatients get a free packet with twenty dollars per day in meal coupons to use in the hospital cafeteria.

Example #3 of RSTUVWX: Independent Interior Design Professional

How does a single person deliver the seven emotions? Again, it is not advised for a single entity (or person) to try to deliver all of them to all customers. It will spread resources too thin, dilute brand, and cause inconsistency. With that said, there are hypothetical ways an independent interior design professional might deliver the seven emotions to her upscale urban clients. These tactics would be equally applicable for many other solopreneur service providers as well.

R = Responsiveness: Sit with upset clients face-to-face for extended discussion. Answer all e-mails or voice mails from clients within two hours of receiving them.

S = Special status: Invite all large-revenue clients to an annual party at a luxurious restaurant.

T = TLC: Learn the six forms of listening (see Chapter Nine) and use daily with clients, as they tend to need all six listening supports at different points in time to feel trust.

U = Uniqueness: Be amenable to special requests; develop relationships with secondary vendors in case the usual offerings do not meet a client's needs.

V = Velocity: Even if the work takes weeks, provide short bursts of completed end products on an ongoing basis. These might include a still photo or video of a completed element of the design work, shared somewhere in the middle of the process. People do not feel comfortable waiting until the end to know results.

W = Wow factor: The end result of the design work should provide the wow factor on its own, but consider adding presentation wow elements, such as music playing in the finished room when the client first views it, decorative paper on which the final report is printed, chilled champagne on a table in the room to toast with the client, etc., to add flair.

X = Extra: Add an unannounced bonus, such as restoration of a wall or door from the adjacent room. (Whatever it is, it should exceed initial expectations.)

The Alternate Mnemonic: All Ts

For those who struggle to remember the items of the RSTUVWX mnemonic, there is an alternate approach based on words that all begin with the letter T.

Responsiveness = Troubles ("listen to my troubles")
Status = Top of the list
TLC = TLC
Uniqueness = Tastes
Velocity = Time
Wow Factor = Ta-da! (magician's exclamation for surprise)
Extra = Tons

* * *

How Now

- *Clarify the company's emotional priorities today, and build an infrastructure to deliver emotion to customers.* Executives, managers, and frontline staff should meet (in a town hall or focus groups) to determine which emotional needs will be the priorities going forward, and then set about executing them. Launch a customer emotion initiative to embed the principles into daily operations. Integrate these emotional priorities into daily operations through training, metrics, feedback, and performance incentives.

- *Executives and managers should observe the retail experience.* Emotional interactions occur in the context of organized spaces, thus observing emotional experiences in the real-life environment validates the intended delivery. What looks good on paper might not materialize in reality. If the intended emotional experiences do not occur (as evidenced by poor sales volume or unhappy customer facial expressions), the issues can be further discussed. In settings where executive presence may prompt staff to act on their best behavior, options such as mystery shoppers or the boss-in-disguise should be considered. This approach can be utilized in environments as varied as banks, retail stores, offices, hospitals, government service centers, and shopping malls.

• *Ask the customers.* Amend current customer feedback processes (e.g., surveys, interviews, evaluation cards) to include the seven emotional parameters. Determine the desired emotional experience of customers and whether the company is delivering it successfully.

Chapter Four:
Hurricane in a Closet

The second of the four emotional interfaces is the team experience. This chapter specifically reviews the nine emotional needs of a team and offers tactics for teams to effectively work together.

Team failures and implosions are commonplace. Every company has stories about "one team that just couldn't get along" or "the rotating door to that department," emanating from poor team culture.

Emotional excellence within teams will take on greater relevance in coming years, as *the team is now the means by which a company generates financial value* in many industries. If a business relies on knowledge integration, service delivery, creative design, or coordinated logistics, it relies on teams as part of the business model.

As task complexity increases in the information age, specialist input is required to achieve intricate results. The one-person show is rare. One person *shouldn't* do everything, because creativity and excellence are supported by multiple minds working together.

For example, a pediatric brain tumor team at a children's hospital might include pediatric oncologists, pediatric neurologists, and pediatric neurosurgeons to provide coordinated care for the patient and family. Filming a major motion picture requires the input of a community of writers, producers, actors, sound/lighting/effects experts, second-unit directors, set designers, and production managers.

Teams should not be idealized, though. Emotional catastrophe can doom any potential earnings from a new product or service. The risk of such team disaster varies by industry, culture, team leadership styles, and a variety of other situational factors, but it is never zero.

Companies make a *choice* to have teams execute their value proposition and thereby generate earnings. It might be impractical to conduct business in a model where a single employee has a do-it-all job description; this reality renders teams a necessity by default. However, team composition should never be thought of as an easy or default practice. Teams are not made of interchangeable machine parts that can be linked, adjusted, or shut down depending on business needs. Bringing humans together to do *anything* is an invitation to elicit the strong emotional potential of the brain, even if some would prefer that emotions be suppressed.

Team Thinking Triggers Team Feeling

As described in Chapter Two, the human brain has numerous juxtapositions of emotional and cognitive centers. The addresses of neurons used in completing analytical and creative business tasks reside next door to emotional houses on the street map of cerebral neighborhoods.

For example, analytical reasoning is housed in the upper parts of the frontal lobe, adjacent to the emotional centers of the inferior frontal lobe. The structure for memory (hippocampus) is in the temporal lobe only a few millimeters away from the processing center for many emotional pathways (amygdala). Neurons responsible for skilled movement (motor cortex) overlap with areas of mirror neurons that allow for physical empathy.

An unexpectedly loud noise or sounds of a raucous party coming from a single house wake up the whole street. Similarly, the activation of one area of the brain for intense thinking engages the adjacent area for feeling. Again, this linkage between cognition and emotion is a survival mechanism for the species; it ensures that great ideas and protective strategies motivate the individual to share the insight and/or experience.

Thus, bringing together neurons to perform work is inherently bringing together neurons to feel. If people think together, the neurological result is that emotions will also enter the team environment. The cognitive horsepower required to generate an innovative solution also tends to generate emotional intensity, which can appear in the form of pride, satisfaction, enjoyment, confidence, defensiveness, need for praise, confrontation, or paranoia.

The burdens of any intense work effort are usually accompanied by periods of stress that may anger, frighten, disappoint, or alienate members within a team. There will be moments in which pressure overwhelms the group and threatens the ability of the team to complete its duties.

Emotions within the team may stay quiet or become vocal, they may unite or divide, they may help to create or destroy. While most teams are somewhere between the extremes of loving families and sworn enemies, the exact combustibility of the team ingredients is always unknown prior to working together. There may be tumultuous upheaval simmering under the veneer of calmness. Putting people together on a team summons an unknown potential, like capturing a hurricane in a closet.

Intense emotional team environments can have a biological effect on team members. In the confined environment of a team room or an executive boardroom, one person's loud disruption raises the heart rate and stress hormone levels in those around him or her; another person's frequent use of humiliation evokes persistent fear and its associated physiological changes. The accumulation of small frictions creates an emotional toxicity within the group and eventually overwhelms the "let's just do the work" reflex. These "team cancers" can include (but are not limited to) apathy, gossip, hypercompetitiveness, humiliation, defensiveness, sabotage, deflection of accountability, perfectionism, and distrust (leading to micromanagement).

Team cancers tend to threaten business outcomes. Emotional failure within a team typically translates to missed deadlines, subpar outputs, and scarred staff that are not adding value to the business enterprise. In rare cases, the disruption of human connectedness can lead to behaviors such as sabotage of a colleague's work or defrauding the company.

It isn't that healthy teams are without conflict. A healthy team vents their frustrations in the occasional tussle and increases tolerance from such moments. Initial yelling is followed by laughing, and then calmly figuring out a way to prevent problems from redeveloping. In contrast, unhealthy teams either avoid directly discussing concerns or don't find resolution from discharging their collective emotional buildup. They fight but nothing gets better because their true emotional needs remain unmet.

Deliver and Decide

Emotional excellence is not about being happy but rather is a state of being capable of accomplishing the team's objectives. A team can appear giddy, but that is irrelevant if it does not deliver results. Conversely, there are some teams with a high degree of observed conflict who still manage to draw upon their residual amount of connectedness to produce in the short term.

A team is ultimately judged in its ability to *deliver* (complete tasks that contribute to operational or financial outcomes) and *decide* (review risks and benefits of potential options and choose among the options). Unresolved team problems can undermine the ability to do either of these.

To *deliver*, a team must be able to define the scope of the work, identify a method of completing that work, assign tasks, and deploy resources to accomplish those tasks. Emotional connectedness enables clarity in each step, while difficulties in establishing team connectedness (i.e., team cancers) will undermine each step. For example, if several team members develop apathy as a consequence of the team leader's punitive style, they may not speak up in critical discussions that determine the work plan and methodology. In another team, unrealistically high expectations make team members hostile toward each other during task assignments. In both examples, the team risks delivering suboptimal results.

To *decide*, teams must specify how they will make decisions (e.g., democracy versus criteria formula), gather required information to make decisions, and discuss how to eliminate options and make a final choice (more on this in Chapter Seven).

Emotional factors often emerge under the stress of the executive process that can lead to poor decisions; these include (but are not limited to) hesitancy to close off options, worry that some detail has been missed, anxiety over who has authority, impatience, avoidance of discussing downside risk, defining individual dominance within the team, and desire for social acceptance among the group. Any of these can distract the team from coming to an optimal answer.

Composition versus Emotional Contribution

The desire to find an exact match for a role or an open position is helpful in team construction, but only to a limited degree. *Teams still fail despite their engineered mix.* By focusing on static individual factors, such as background, experience, or personality type, you will ignore the dynamic patterns of group emotional behaviors.

Good composition might decrease the risk of emotional disruption, but only team members' willingness to serve in *emotional roles* can fully mitigate disruptive tendencies. Specific personality types or backgrounds are neither sufficient nor necessary to successful teams; teams thrive when individual members understand the dynamics within the group and execute certain roles to meet emotional needs.

There are nine emotional needs within a team. Each team member has the duty to contribute these for the group's success: progress (achievement), peace, nurturance, inspiration, inclusion, imagination (excitement of possibility), gratitude, fun, and friendship.

These nine team emotional needs are *not the same as the seven categories of customer emotional experiences.* The relationship is entirely different. With customers there is a transactional situation of exchanging needs for value, while teamwork is a cooperative effort formed on the basis of shared common goals. Thus, there are different emotional needs required for success.

To construct and maintain the emotionally engaged team, *someone* on the team must be able to promote each of these nine emotional connection factors. Team construction should focus on determining who could provide each of the nine rather than assuming people are static categories of personality. Two similar candidates might have very different tendencies toward which emotional contributions they'll make to a team environment.

Each emotional contribution is not a weekly must-do obligation, but a responsibility for looking out within the team. The office's fire marshal will hopefully never actually have to vacate the premises, but it's good to know who will be acting as the fire marshal ahead of time should things get hot. Similarly, the need for an "inspirer" to keep the group focused on potential impact may not arise, but it is important to know who will be playing such a role in case it is needed.

Imagine nine guards along a strategic 360-degree circular fort, spread 40 degrees apart from each other. Each of the nine is a just-in-case protector, called into action only when an enemy force from a particular trajectory threatens the team. Each guard may never be called on to do battle but must be ready should the call come. For example, in a particular team no one feels excited about the unglamorous role to ensure peace, but someone still needs to take on the role. The person who takes on the role of ensuring peace certainly does not need to go to an extreme, such as leading hand-holding sessions supported by frequent queries about whether feelings have been hurt. Rather, he or she must be ready to recognize strife when it arises and pursue the appropriate measures to address it.

Any team member (junior or leader, regardless of personality type) might play any of these nine roles. There might be one person accepting four of them, or four people overlapping on one of them.

Leaders must ensure that the team members meet all nine needs. This might include role delegation to junior members of the team or mentoring others to do so. For example, "Javier, there is no one on the team who is ensuring we are having enough fun. I'm appointing you to be the 'cruise director' to bring some levity to the team room. Come up with something hilarious for us to do on Monday afternoons for thirty minutes as a group. Let's turn Mondays into Fundays."

If the leader senses that one of the nine needs is lacking, then she should step forward to provide that to the team even if it is not a naturally comfortable position for her. Jane might not normally be inclined toward expressing gratitude, for example, but she might need to offer thanks to a fatigued team that is losing morale with no one else playing that particular role.

Nine Funny Rooms in a Corporate Hallway

The nine needs are not a menu from which a team can pick only one as their favorite. To comically illustrate how a team would look if it were only addressing one need, imagine a long hallway near the top floor of a huge skyscraper. The hallway has nine small conference rooms, each with a team of people working on a business issue, using whiteboards and laptops. Scattered report binders and documents are strewn across tables, as they are midway through their current initiative.

The peculiarity about this hallway is that each of the teams has only one of the nine emotional team needs being addressed by the team members; in each room various talents, titles, and types are present, but the groups are only bound (sadly) by one emotional force.

In room one, *progress* is the single dominant factor. While the team members are working furiously to complete the tasks, they cannot maintain momentum, as multiple people eagerly take turns to jump up to the whiteboard checklist and cross items off. They are as excited about documenting progress as making it.

In room two, *peace* is the key emotional factor. Team members are working intensively but are slowed by the need to phrase every idea in a nonconfrontational manner and then asking each other, "Did you feel okay about how that was stated?" In the hallway, the team leader is facilitating diplomatic negotiations between two members of the team who had a fight the day before.

In room three, *nurturance* guides the team's efforts. Crumbs from the red velvet cupcakes the leader brought in are sprinkled among papers and laptop keyboards. One of the staff is mentoring the two junior associates in one corner of the room in time management skills while the rest of the team continues to work on the project. There is an enormous banner over the door that says, "Listen Today, Lead Tomorrow."

In room four, *inspiration* is the emotional paradigm. Team members are deeply entrenched in the data but "come up for ten thousand-foot air" repeatedly. They respond with wild cheering at the junior analyst's single arithmetic calculation. The leader smiles and asks hourly, "Isn't it amazing what we can do on this team? We are having so much impact!"

In room five, *inclusion* is the priority. After each idea has been presented, all other members of the team offer feedback. Everyone's input is needed on every issue. They are planning to offer their final document with four supplemental minority reports in order to include everyone.

In room six, *imagination* is the fuel for the group's fire. Every idea is met with "X sounds good, but let's build on that and add Y and Z too!" At one point, there is talk of using a live zebra, a decommissioned army helicopter, and a violin quartet to demonstrate the financial capital concepts within their presentation to the steering committee.

In room seven, one can easily witness *gratitude*. Mixed in with the binders of papers are small handwritten notes of appreciation between team members. The leader ends the two-hour meeting twenty minutes early in order to have enough time to recognize the contributions of each person in that meeting. Some inquire whether hourly appreciations would be more appropriate.

In room eight, *fun* is the name of the game. Team members have decorated the conference room with a Caribbean theme along with dance music playing in the background. When a team member offers criticism to the prior week's deliverable, the others call her a "party pooper."

In room nine, *friendship* connects the team to each other. The group begins the Monday meeting by listening to what everyone did over the weekend. When one team member had an unfortunate interaction with a traffic policeman on his way to work, each teammate makes sure to offer him a hug before resuming work discussions.

None of these rooms is a desirable environment (although some may sound eerily familiar). Meeting emotional needs must *empower* the work of a team (i.e., deliver and decide) and never *become* the work of the team, as in these examples.

Without someone on the team who is responsible for injecting the right degree of each of the nine emotions at the right time, the group's stresses, conflicts, and risk of failure will destructively grow.

The Nine Needs

On the menu of most Indian restaurants is a popular item called *navratan korma*, a curry mix of multiple vegetables and spices. The name literally translates to "nine jewels." Without each of the ingredients, the dish loses its distinctive flavor. All nine are required, and the blend of having just enough of each ingredient makes it a successful entrée. The same goes for a team. For different "working palates" there might be a desire for more of one emotion compared with another, but all nine of the ingredients are relevant to addressing a potential stumbling block to the team's eventual success. The team must balance the nine needs according to its business objectives; the team can become dysfunctional with the wrong balance of roles being played (too much of this, not enough of that).

Progress. Herds in all species are aware of impending disruption; they disperse quickly when disaster is imminent. Humans also have such instinctive repulsion to disorder. Within every team, there will be moments where anxiety rises in relation to chaos or missed milestones; people worry that they're not moving fast enough and that failure is possible. People fear potential chaos, anarchy, and unmet expectations. In these moments, someone on the team who can articulate (visually or verbally) what has been achieved will help the team by restoring a sense of healthy progress and stability. She provides a sense of accomplishment to the group by the use of regular scorecards, checklists, and status updates. (Incidentally, these actions also allow for effective upward management of nervous senior executives or board members who are concerned with team progress.)

Peace. Threats trigger attack behaviors. Teams are frequently derailed when individual differences in style, communications, or agendas come into angry confrontation. For a team to minimize this potential, someone needs to be a peacemaker who can smooth over hurt emotions and suggest methods to resolve disputes. Such a diplomat may work overtly or off-line. He requires abilities such as listening, reassuring, reframing, and providing feedback to maintain civility.

Nurturance. Survival is supported by actions such as mentorship, nourishment, resuscitation, and encouragement. Particularly for long-term efforts that have a tendency to deplete emotional energy like exhaustive marathons, teams need someone who will sustain them when they are vulnerable. This role involves being on the lookout for others who appear overwhelmed or withdrawn. Reassurance through comments like "Don't worry, I've seen this before and we'll get through it" provides emotional fuel to continue with intense work. Periodic treats such as doughnuts or cake demonstrate the physical side of nurturance; periodic "emotional treats," such as unsolicited compliments and coaching, offer the emotional side of nurturance to teammates.

Inspiration. A grand vision—"reaching for the stars"—draws teams together and energizes them. Inspired action and inspired language stimulate the emotional brain; it is the reason altruistic descriptions often evoke tears and passion. We look to political or spiritual leaders to do this in speeches; on a team, anyone can do it through an emphasis on values or the impact of the team's work. Teams require someone who pushes for the team to achieve the most noble, impressive, groundbreaking, or dramatic outcome possible. Without someone playing this role, groups adopt the emotional disengagement that accompanies mediocrity.

Inclusion. On some teams, dominant voices drown out the other voices on the team. A team of six may feel like a team of only two voices accompanied by four silent observers. A lack of passion for the work and feeling undervalued may take the form of apathy, sadness, withdrawal, or other appearances of disengagement from others. Someone on the team must periodically scan the room to assess whether everyone has been heard and their views acknowledged. This might be done by establishing discussion practices for every person to say something or by simply asking, "Hey, Susie, you're the newest member of the group. Do you agree with the team on this?" The team member who ensures inclusion might conduct off-line conversations to boost people's confidence and create opportunities so that every team member has a chance to shine. Each person is energized when he or she can say, "I'm part of something bigger than myself." Inclusion also implies listening to the more cynical (and less popular) members of the group who emphasize risks and the downside of potential actions. No teammate left behind.

Imagination. Teams can become emotionally disengaged if their work tasks become too monotonous or routine. Results suffer as group members simply perform without passion. One element of maintaining freshness in a team's work is asking atypical questions, which forces the emotional brain to see the situation as new and creative. When the group is forced to think together because of an unorthodox approach, the group sees itself as more unified. The "progress of thought" is often as motivating as the progress of results. Children play for hours with minimal materials if they can imagine their surroundings as something extraordinary. Big thinking often goes with big emotion.

Gratitude. For some team members, acknowledgment of their performance and contribution is emotionally enriching and keeps them engaged. When they receive appreciation from their supervisor for doing something superlative, they remember it vividly. It keeps them motivated to continue working hard. (Albeit, gratitude that is formulaic or insincere has no effect.) In contrast, the leader who says, "If you don't hear anything from me, assume you're doing fine," is ignoring the emotional importance of recognizing contributions. Gratitude can be written, spoken, demonstrated by small gifts, or even communicated through a simple thumbs-up gesture.

Fun. Animals play, and babies laugh; people watch millions of viral videos of both as entertainment. It is inherent to human existence that fun be a part of life, even if fun has traditionally been viewed as inappropriate in some workplaces. Injecting a dose of humor, frivolity, or playfulness can rejuvenate (translation: "make young again") the ethos of a team. This can be done by someone who tells a joke, performs a humorous song, or organizes a five-minute "energizer game" to begin the day. Some managers will include silly prizes for the highest performers (e.g., tiny trophies or action figures of superheroes) in sales team meetings; laughter and applause can emotionally reinforce excellence.

Friendship. Somewhere in our professional development we are taught that there should be a wall between coworkers and friends. Yet in the context of a team, this wall may be removed to improve the team dynamics. People who build spreadsheets together can play golf together too. Even if close personal connection is not desired, recognition of a personal event is typically appreciated (e.g., a birthday card). The person assigned to this need might provide a reassuring phone call during the evening if he senses a team member has had a terrible day at work. Teams can also establish working friendships by having meals together with a "no shop talk" rule, or scheduling a once-a-month team event in the evening.

Team Need	Keith, Team Leader	Jennifer	Indira	Horatio
Progress		●		
Peace			●	
Nurturance	●		●	
Inspiration				●
Inclusion				●
Imagination				●
Gratitude			●	
Fun	●	●	●	●
Friendship			●	

Team Need	Grace, Team Leader	Francesca	Eleanor	Donna
Progress	●			
Peace	●			
Nurturance	●			
Inspiration	●			
Inclusion	●			
Imagination	●			
Gratitude			●	
Fun		●		
Friendship				●

Examples of team emotional role distribution

Individual people vary as to their desire for these nine elements within a group (e.g., Joe needs seven of them to feel connected, Susie needs only four). Some may actually be a "turn off" if done excessively or incorrectly. The challenge for teams is to emotionally contribute somewhere between the barely adequate minimum and the undesirable maximum.

Even if the entire team were to agree up front to the irrelevance of one of the nine and eliminate it from the list, it should not be eliminated entirely. Unforeseen later changes in the team's targets or broader company circumstances might elevate its necessity. Sufficiently ensuring all nine within the team is a matter of prevention.

Take the Charging Foul

Successful teams also maintain an important habit: the confrontation of unpopular truth.

When there is a serious problem within a team, the individual(s) responsible for ensuring a particular emotional need must speak up (e.g., "This team has low morale because we are attacking each other instead of maintaining peace"). But what if team members are afraid to point out the problem to the group or the leader? It will always be easier to avoid actions that carry personal risk; it is much simpler to hope problems dissolve on their own. Nonetheless, denial of an issue is rarely the best approach to dealing with predicaments.

This avoidance response is analogous to the challenge faced by basketball players on defense. When an opponent has the ball and is dribbling quickly with momentum to the basket, the last defensive player has to step in front of the moving offensive player. If the defensive player has clearly established his position and gets knocked down, then the shooter is charged with an offensive foul and commits a violation. The ball is then given over to the defense. The defensive player's splendid action in this case is called "taking a charge" and is usually lauded by teammates. Coaches also admire it greatly. It is a painful way to help teammates though, as it typically implies accepting a forceful blow to the unprotected chest and abdomen and hitting the ground with significant kinetic energy. It hurts, but it helps the team.

When speaking uncomfortable truth to a single teammate or the broader team, the experience feels the same as taking a charge. It will hurt but will have benefits for the team. Calling attention to problems is a needed role for everyone on the team but is not an easy role to embrace.

The anxiety and apprehension that accompanies the act of brutal honesty ("disclosure discomfort") may spring from multiple internal fears or worries.

"I am afraid to say something directly to someone on the team because:

1. It says something negative about me and redefines my identity" (e.g., *I am rude, I am a whistleblower*).
2. "It may lead to an immediately painful consequence" (e.g., *retaliation, yelling, violence, criticism of me*).
3. "It may lead to a longer-term threat to me" (e.g., *exclusion from group connectedness, future sabotage of my work, retribution on my performance review*)
4. "It may damage my interactions/relationships" (e.g., *the person will be offended, we're no longer friends*)
5. "It may actually worsen the situation" (e.g., *telling someone he is apathetic may make him more apathetic, telling someone he or she is inappropriate may make him or her more inappropriate*)

All of these factors may be true in particular situations and should be carefully considered in prior to raising a discussion of threats to the team. *It is not always the right decision to bluntly bring up problems to others.* The decision algorithm must compare pros and cons of continuing the current state versus making changes.

The analytical calculation of whether to say something directly may lead to a yes or no, favoring direct disclosure or favoring some other approach to problem resolution. *What must be kept out of the equation is your internal fear present in the moment.* You must be willing to take a charge.

Confronting a difficult circumstance is best done by an invitation to engage in direct, difficult conversation. For example, if you were to confront your boss Dieter about something he is doing that is detrimental to the team, you might say, "Dieter, I feel compelled to say something that you may not want to hear." You then pause for one full second for this to sink in. "Your [appearance/behavior/mind-set] makes me [emotional adjective] and is affecting the team." You pause again for this to sink in. "Can we discuss this now or at a later hour?"

To adequately prepare for this confrontation, prepare your exact three sentences in advance. Otherwise, your anxiety may be overwhelmingly intense and your words will not flow appropriately. Some people practice in front of a mirror, others record their voice and listen to it, and still others prefer a live partner to practice with who can provide feedback on their delivery style.

One common mistake in speaking truth to individuals who scare us is to gradually introduce the topic rather than directly stating it. Most people have had the uncomfortable experience of someone coming to them, smiling and asking how they are doing, then engage in frivolous chit-chat, only to "drop the bomb" on them a few moments later. Most people can intuitively surmise that something negative is to follow when a sugary sweet introduction is presented; the gradual introduction actually backfires because it allows time for emotional defenses to mount and the receiver to build antagonism about a dishonest introduction. If there is something difficult to say, following the candid three-sentence style above allows the receiver some freedom to defer but does not generate defensiveness.

* * *

How Now

Team deterioration and implosion is not inevitable. Speaking candidly about emotional roles and emotional problems has the potential to *prevent* problems from arising or worsening. Companies can implement some immediate tactics to improve team functioning.

- *Compose teams based on emotional contributions.* As a team is forming or considering a new addition, potential candidates should be interviewed about how they could contribute to the nine emotional needs, not just their relevant experience. "How would you help solve a deficit of imagination in a team?" might be an interview question, for example. As leaders approach the kickoff of a team initiative, each of the nine roles must be clear ("gratitude guy," "progress pusher," "diplomat," etc.).

- *Develop a team charter document (and discuss).* A team charter is a document that is developed through team discussion at the beginning of a project (or adapted as new members enter the team). The discussion/ document delineates the emotional priorities of the team. Team members agree to which of the nine needs they will commit to preserving for the group. The exact distribution of roles and responsibilities may evolve over time, but the mere act of having the discussion calls attention to the needs so that they are not forgotten. The initial discussion agenda can include overall goals, metrics, working calendar, group norms, and the individual commitments to ensuring the nine needs.

- *Track the team's emotional barometer.* Just as companies continuously track operational equipment and financial resources to catch problems early, they should also monitor the emotional needs of the team by gathering team feedback on a regular basis. Periodic anonymous surveys about team performance and team dynamics can provide additional insights into the team's ability to meet objectives. Teams can identify and deal with emerging issues early, before they escalate into destructive cancers.

- *Make facilitators for emotional discussion mandatory.* Left to their own choice, teams will rarely want to begin a project with discussion of emotions or conflict prevention. In order to appear results-oriented to their peers and superiors, team members will want to jump quickly into work planning and problem solving. They will see emotional discussion as a waste of time that will only make them uncomfortable. The only way the company can ensure healthy teams is to require a facilitator (from HR or an external firm) to guide such a discussion at team kickoffs, when launching a project initiative or new effort. Once this is established as a company expectation (and budgeted for), the initial resistance will diminish in favor of emotional rigor as a mechanism for team success.

- *Prepare a plan B.* Even with careful attention to the nine needs, there may be situations where team functioning deteriorates rapidly due to unforeseen factors. Teams should identify up front their "plan B" if such a scenario were to occur. What can the group do if things are stuck in a bad place? Plan B options include delegating contentious decisions upward to organizational superiors, suspending the team's work for a day to openly express current frustrations, engaging a consultant/mediator to work with the team, temporarily reassigning members to or from the team, and revisiting the need for the team to exist at all (i.e., could the company achieve the desired outcome through an alternate organizational unit?).

Chapter Five:
Get on the Same Page Now

The third of the four emotional interfaces is coexistence with oppositional parties. This chapter describes several frameworks for assessing and addressing stakeholder conflicts.

Us versus them. Nothing emboldens a group more than a menace, whether individual villain or evil empire. We coalesce to overcome enemies.

When we perceive enemies are within our business, we begin to paint colleagues in unfavorable hues. We make our *co*-lleague the *foe*-lleague. Unmet business expectations are too often blamed on the actions of others in the same company rather than shifts in the market, availability of capital, globalization, or other forces beyond the control of the company. Macroeconomics is too complicated to be the villain, so fault is placed down the hall.

For example, when revenue is down, the employees in sales blame marketing, who blame purchasing, who blame finance, who blame R&D, who blame production, who blame sales. When there is an operational bottleneck in a hospital, staff in the emergency room blame the ICU, who blame radiology, who blame the operating room, who blame the emergency room. We point a finger at the most nearby culprit rather than something amorphous like "the system," even though it may be that overarching system that has led to the problems.

Exacerbating internal strife is the measurement and rewarding of targets that set one unit of a company as rivals against another. Rather than aligning on a set of mutually beneficial goals, rewarding performance in relative terms (e.g., the top R&D site gets bigger bonuses) motivates business units to wrongly view internal partners as competitors.

Ubiquitous Persistent Threat

A threat is anything that has the potential to disrupt, detract, deny, or destroy. A violent attacker poses a threat, but so does the sinister colleague who undermines or sabotages coworkers in order to make a favorable impression on the boss.

The physiologic underpinning of human resilience to threats is the catecholamine cascade, often called the fight-or-flight response. When encountering danger, the hormones epinephrine and norepinephrine trigger a litany of physiological changes throughout the body, including shifts in heart rate, respiration, pupil size, gastrointestinal motility, and blood glucose levels. Stress hormones, including cortisol, supplement this response, allowing the body to be ready for a fight against impending threats. For completeness, the fight-or-flight response should be amended to include the third reflexive response of "freeze," avoiding detection by minimal movement in the face of impending harm. Both physical and emotional threats can trigger the fight-flight-freeze hormonal/neurological responses.

There are two situations for which this elegant physiology is *wrongly* suited as a form of resilience: (1) overwhelming assault to the entire nervous system and (2) ubiquitous persistent threat that lasts beyond a few moments.

Overwhelming assaults to the entire nervous system (e.g., battlefield explosions, rape, mugging) involve a simultaneous *sensory* shock (smell, sound, touch, and sight) with *emotional* shocks (terror and helplessness). Human resiliency is often inadequate to deal with such intense combined sensory/emotional attacks, and post-traumatic stress disorder (PTSD) is the common residual scar. Academic research has paid great attention to such onslaughts, but fortunately they are not common to the everyday business environment.

In contrast, the second form of nervous system insult is found commonly in businesses all over the world. Ubiquitous persistent threat (UPT) is a situational circumstance where a *threat remains in place over time,* because active confrontation is either unwarranted or undesirable. Internal physiology primes the body for a fight, but the fight doesn't come. Yet, the hormones keep releasing and building up within the body, because the threat remains. If the danger is the cruel boss or the sinister other department, the threat seems to be everywhere every day. Thus, it is ubiquitous and persistent. Going to work feels like going to war, with workers' physiology primed for battle against others in the office.

Groups may feel threatened by other groups over any number of issues, but they tend to be most polarized around *items* (budget resources, equipment, etc.), *ideals* (mission, goals, aspirations, the way we work, etc.), or *identities* (defining who is the leader and who stays employed if things get worse). I discuss these three sources of threat in more detail in Chapter Ten. In the setting of UPT, all three of these polarizing issues may be present among stakeholder groups in conflict.

At first, UPT may provoke a few minor behavioral reactions, such as nervousness or avoidance of the perceived villain. Over time, there may be more physiological effects, such as headaches, sleeplessness, muscular aches, gastrointestinal discomfort, or jitteriness. (As a matter of distinction, clinical depression has some similarities to this list but manifests with alternate symptoms, including unprovoked crying, changes in sex drive and hunger, and an inability to find pleasure.)

Eventually, UPT undermines emotional brain reactions, thereby lessening individual trust and engagement with colleagues. This appears outwardly as apathy, avoidance, irritability, and paranoia.

Long-term UPT has the potential to warp group perceptions, as the chronic overload of the stress hormones begins to alter group neurophysiology. It provokes some groups into extreme reactions of an aggressive nature, such as the sectarian sabotage between divisions of the same religion. Politicians and political parties gradually shift from bipartisan spirit to being cynical of the other side's underlying motives and doubting their inherent goodness. When threat is believed to be everywhere, enemies begin to include people with nearly identical backgrounds, values, income class, and aspirations.

The ring of trust grows smaller with time as UPT warps perceptions. At first a national border separates the enemy; the threat may come from a different corporate vice president. Then distrust infects minds within the borders of the same business unit. Eventually the threat is seen in the same office, perhaps even the same team. UPT may be informally thought of as office politics or backstabbing; the effect of shrinking trust is dangerous regardless of its name.

Management activities do not normally take UPT into consideration despite its potential to derail progress. Standard operating procedures, job descriptions, and strategic plans typically assume that workers will conduct themselves in a fully aligned and synchronized manner, but that is not always the case. "I can't get my report done because I'm still waiting for that data from the other department" is an all-too-common utterance. Following a merger, individuals in the incumbent and acquired organizations often take significant time to blend in with the other entity, as they were once the competitor;

this distrust potentially nullifies the financial aims of the acquisition.

In a fraction of cases, UPT is triggered because of a gradually shrinking financial outlook for the company. Items, ideals, and identities are all sources of friction. If there isn't healthy demand for a company's products, then naturally there are smaller budgets, smaller aspirations, and fewer roles for people to play. Rivals will be fighting over resources and spans of control that are too small to be sufficient if they would attempt to share them. In such cases, no amount of insightful diagnostics or conflict mediation will change the fact that there just isn't enough to go around. The company needs to find a new equilibrium of simpler organizational structure and size; a larger number was correct for a different time, but times have changed.

Given that value creation is dependent on aligned and synchronized execution among many internal stakeholders, inability to align or synchronize leads to lost earnings. Groups are not on the same page, and it impacts the way business is conducted.

UPT Earnings Drainers

In physics, when two objects are in motion and come into physical contact, a certain proportion of their combined energy can be lost in the form of heat, light, or sound (or all three). Such "frictional loss" decreases the amount of energy remaining in either object. Organizations of all sizes encounter the same frictional loss phenomena when different business units, all moving with a high degree of energy, come into contact with each other and do not collaborate smoothly. UPT causes frictional losses at thousands of daily interaction points within a company.

Of all the links between emotion and financial performance, the most "invisible" and the one that can be most insidious in its ability to annihilate an enterprise is the impact of UPT on operations and earnings.

Any business with more than one employee requires people to trust each other to perform the basic operations of the business. A restaurant owner has to trust that workers are not damaging the property, spitting in the food, or stealing from the register. A regional network of charitable entities has to trust that local staff will honestly report donations without embezzlement. A multinational conglomerate has internal audit controls to track billions of dollars but still must trust that the matrix reporting system between geography leaders and product leaders will result in benefits rather than battles.

Lost earnings are the result of distrust, avoidance, and paranoia. In the absence of trust, a warped sense of threat (including believing that the destruction of a colleague increases the probability of one's own promotion) underlies behaviors that pose operational and financial risk to the company.

Consider a hypothetical example of a European high-tech manufacturer seeing tremendous revenue growth in China. The three traditional product-based business units (BUs) must now adapt because the company has added a fourth "China BU" that cuts across products but has sole ownership of that geographic market. The senior leadership's logical rationale to the three product BU leaders is that managing the customer segments and possessing the specialized knowledge to operate in China requires a separate new BU. The product BU leaders smile to their CEO but then drag their feet in helping the fourth BU achieve its objectives. They sense their own compensation, promotion trajectories, and authority will be diluted as a result of a fourth BU. They gently inform their subordinates of their displeasure with the new China group, and that subtle signal slows down numerous operational handoffs. Data are not transmitted quickly when a request comes from China, knowledge management systems "accidentally" exclude China staff from accessing any company intelligence, and the China

BU leader is never invited to teleconferences with the three product BU leaders. Even if the Chinese market represents a huge growth opportunity, will this company be able to ensure growth with these internal conditions?

UPT drains earnings from a company a drop at a time, in mechanisms that happen invisibly and insidiously:

1. Employees spend time revising, reworking, and redoing value-adding tasks because of their avoidance to communicate alignment up front.
2. Employees spend time in bureaucratic cover-your-a** (CYA) activities rather than their value-adding core functions.
3. Employees delay internal transfer of data, best practices, and customer relationship messaging due to paranoia of what will be done with particular information by other internal groups.
4. Leaders spend inordinate time in closed-door lobbying or negotiating for internal resources rather than creating value.
5. In rare cases, employees engage in sabotaging reputations or performance of other units of the company (especially if KPIs/incentives are based on comparative performance).

These five frictional losses can easily absorb multiple hours of employee effort per week and instigate missed sales handoffs on a repeated basis.

It would be highly unlikely to find all five of these UPT earnings drainers at a company. If such a terrible scenario existed, the company would not survive very long. Revenue generation activities would be impossible to synchronize, and service problems would make existing customers flee for greener pastures. Nonetheless, even one of the five revenue-draining behaviors can drag down earnings in any company by the punitive weight of distrust.

Symptom Checklist: Oppositional Behaviors

While UPT may serve as a useful concept to understand the root causes of misaligned activities within a business, it is difficult to directly observe. Even when asked via anonymous survey, people may feel compelled to report positive interactions when fractured relations are the actual conditions on the ground. The five revenue drainers of UPT (rework, CYA, handoff delays, resource politics, and sabotage) are not subjects that people freely discuss with senior management. Thus, leaders must look for alternate observable symptom behaviors that indicate problems with alignment, trust, and the ability to work collaboratively.

The following checklist represents *nine observable patterns of distrust* among oppositional stakeholders that indicate UPT is likely present. Unlike generic employee surveys or interviews that inquire about individual mind-sets, this list is an observation tool for a neutral party (e.g., senior leader from another department or externally engaged mediator) to use as part of a formal assessment that includes interviews and/or focus groups.

1. *We reinvent the wheel.* Companies with UPT conduct duplicative research, analytics, product development, sales calls, and other resource-intensive efforts, because "the right hand has no idea what the left hand is doing."
2. *Decisions are not final.* The etymology of the word "decision" comes from the same root as "incision"— the latter means *to cut into,* the former means *to cut off,* as in "cutting off" further deliberation. Yet in an organization burdened with oppositional strife,

decisions are continually revisited as small power shifts lead to back-and-forth jockeying between distrustful parties. Decisions seem more like temporary preferences than firm agreements to act. Unpopular decisions are responded to with inaction accompanied by a wait-and-see attitude.

3. *There is a machinelike work environment.* If UPT is present, then there is minimal socializing (e.g., no friendly chats with colleagues over a cup of coffee). People do not lower their guard for fear of being perceived as goofing off for even a moment. Leaving one's desk for lunch is considered weak. Group activities, such as meetings or conference calls, begin without polite social graces.

4. *Units are isolated.* People work physically and/or emotionally separated when UPT is present. There is little exchange except for transactional needs. Interaction across divisions or functions is rare. Even if a department promotes social cohesiveness among its own staff, people are cold toward other parts of the company. Leaders frown upon engagement across silo walls.

5. *People hoard secrets.* UPT drives people to hoard information so colleagues won't have access to it. Workers must overcome multiple hurdles to share information, even if it delays service to customers. Everything is kept on a need-to-know basis, as if espionage is occurring. There are opaque communications rather than open talks. A culture of secrets is difficult to detect, as even the most guarded of executives may have a smiling veneer.

6. *There is no plan B.* Whether in regard to worst-case business forecasts or succession planning, UPT prevents enterprise-wide risks from being discussed because of distrust of other units and leaders.

Individual departments and units may diligently assess risks, but cross-department discussions do not occur because leaders fear of how they will be perceived relative to others.

7. *Enthusiasm is extinguished.* UPT and oppositional culture make a working environment emotionally painful. It is tiring to always be in a state of threat. From the perspective of observable behaviors, people do not smile, and they might sigh and cry at their desks. They frequently look for escapes to avoid the work environment, such as attending out-of-office meetings and a significantly higher-than-average sickness rate. There is a collective "get me out of here" feeling.

8. *Overproduction is a sign of fear.* If a group is always worried about how they will be perceived, they will overproduce documents and evidence of activity. UPT prompts document writing and activity reports far beyond what is necessary—for example, producing forty pages for a thirty-minute meeting "just in case," postponing actual work that needs to get done. The group includes a large number of insecure overachievers. Regarding communications, even short e-mails are copied to fifty people so that everyone who is remotely affected (just in case) cannot later say, "I wasn't in the loop" (even though this floods everyone's e-mail inbox with irrelevant things to review as a result).

9. *Conflict is clumsy.* Rather than resolving problems collaboratively through compromise, UPT makes people unstable. They yell and scream and get personal. Frustration boils over and/or groups avoid each other for significant periods of time based on a previous bad encounter. Other groups with UPT approach conflict in a clumsy avoidant manner,

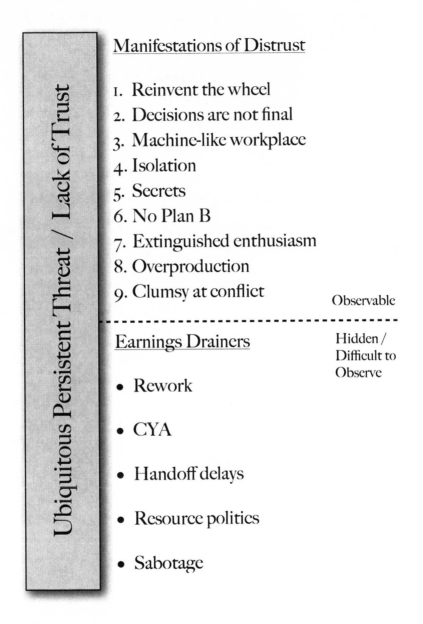

Ubiquitous Persistent Threat / Lack of Trust

Manifestations of Distrust

1. Reinvent the wheel
2. Decisions are not final
3. Machine-like workplace
4. Isolation
5. Secrets
6. No Plan B
7. Extinguished enthusiasm
8. Overproduction
9. Clumsy at conflict

Observable

- -

Earnings Drainers

Hidden /
Difficult to
Observe

- Rework

- CYA

- Handoff delays

- Resource politics

- Sabotage

Observable and Unobservable elements of UPT

where people don't speak directly about a problem but rather generate numerous lengthy e-mails to give the false appearance of civility.

A company can survive if only a few of these checklist items are present. The more checklist symptoms present, the more likely that earnings/value creation is inhibited. To maximize the ability of the enterprise to create earnings, groups must get on the same page now.

Reducing the Business Impact of Opposition

In earlier chapters, I defined two different forms of emotional relationships: (1) transactional relationships with customers, within which seven emotional needs (RSTUVWX) create connection, and (2) team relationships defined by common aspirations, with nine emotional needs required for maintaining connectedness to decide and deliver.

Oppositional stakeholder parties represent a third category of situational relationships, different from either customers or teams. A UPT environment within a company makes shared aspirations unlikely. *Coexistence* might be the best a group can hope for under tense circumstances, with a goal of minimizing the business impact of opposition.

This can be done via four approaches:

1. Strategies/policies that prevent the formation of structural opposition in the organization
2. Decoupling the link between UPT and business practices through operational changes
3. Redefining the paradigm of success with opposition
4. Fixing emotional relationships between oppositional parties (reduce the degree of confrontation)

First, in regard to *prevention*, it is naive to believe that UPT can be entirely eliminated. Oppositional parties in a battle for items, ideals, or identity are often intensely loyal to their agendas; these agendas are borne from uncertain business conditions and very tangible concerns, such as risks, scarcity, and access to power. Nonetheless, some corporate HR strategies can reduce infighting: compensation based on overall company results, performance evaluations that include collaboration behavioral objectives, and 360-degree feedback processes tied to promotions. Decision making can also be adapted to prevent UPT, by defining exact circumstances where units within the company should align. Knowing how and when specific controversial decisions will be made prevents the decision from being politicized. Chapter Eight also discusses ways of "changing the oil" to prevent organizational distress.

Second, breaking the link between UPT and business practices requires *"decoupling."* A company can redesign production-service processes such that the business runs efficiently in spite of antagonism and tensions. In other words, companies should implement procedures that minimize the impact of conflicted humans. Specific decoupling tactics include software automation of some activities, consolidation of organizational units doing similar activities to avoid "overlap friction," and outsourcing selected business activities that promote internal strife (i.e., "We can't do it internally without fighting so let's give it to a third party"). Of course, any of these approaches involves considerable investment of staff time, funds, and management attention to enact.

Third, redefining the paradigm of success involves *adopting an attitude of compromise* into negotiation, which is very difficult. Compromise never ends with the sides completely happy. Each party must define what outcomes they fundamentally want to see achieved and then revisit options they would be alternately willing to accept. The all-or-none outcome ("We get everything we want, and they get nothing") rarely happens unless a cataclysmic event occurs; resources expended waiting for the other side to fall will be self-destructive in the meanwhile. Win-win situations are theoretically desirable but not always immediately available. Rather, one of three alternate mind-sets has to be acceptable: (1) *grand exchange*, where losing on an outcome is balanced by winning on an entirely unrelated second outcome, (2) *mosaic* of winning pieces ("We both get partial victories"), or (3) the *nuclear option* that settles on a path that leaves everyone having lost something in the process.

For example, if two product-based business units within a conglomerate were locked in a stalemate over the five-year R&D budget, the three compromise mind-sets of exchange, mosaic, and nuclear options could be applied: (1) Group A gets the much bigger R&D budget, but Group B gets vastly more flexibility in purchasing vendor decisions; (2) Group A gets the larger chunk for R&D equipment and materials, while Group B gets the larger chunk for R&D specialist labor; or (3) the R&D budget will be *combined* for the two groups, and a neutral panel will appropriate the funds.

As a second example, if there was a stubborn showdown between the Green Party and Orange Party within a national parliament about how to finance health-care coverage for the elderly, then (1) the Green Party wins control over elderly health-care coverage, but the Orange Party gets to control military spending; (2) the Green Party defines elderly hospital costs while the Orange Party defines elderly outpatient and medication costs; or (3) the country switches from an insurance model of health care to a nationalized/socialized network of physicians and facilities. None of these compromises creates harmony, but they offer an equilibrium of partial victories to both sides.

Fourth, fixing relationships between oppositional parties can be attempted using a variety of *diplomatic and relationship-*

building tactics (the upcoming seven social Fs list). Hostile parties must "get over it" and redefine their relationship.

Moving beyond Fight-or-Flight-or-Freeze: The Seven Social Fs

Fight, flight, and freeze are biologically inborn instincts to survive threats from predators and other external lethal agents, but they also are provoked by stresses in the modern business environment. To summarize these three (for both individuals *and* groups):

Fight = physical or verbal aggression
Flight = run away, isolate, avoid
Freeze = don't do anything, hope the threat goes away

The limitation of these "primitive F" group responses is that they minimize human connectedness rather than enhancing it. They are not useful in a business conflict, when it isn't a realistic option of punching the supervisor you don't like or running away as fast as you can out of the office parking lot.

There are seven additional "social Fs" that can assist oppositional parties within an organization. Though simple and logical, each requires a high willingness to be vulnerable to the other party for progress to occur.

The first of these new Fs is philosophical: *forgiveness*. If we perceive another group as a threat, then it becomes impossible to lower emotional defenses to work together. Forgiveness is a conscious decision to remove these preconceptions of threat and start anew. To implement this, in whatever written or verbal manner is appropriate, a group indicates that previous tension is no longer an impediment to working together. For example, a joint meeting at a neutral location begins with the opening statement, "In the past, our two departments did not see eye to eye, and we've all been hurt by that. Today we're starting a new chapter of shared accountability for results."

Flowers is the second new F. To fix the troubled linkage between two oppositional parties, bring a gift as a peace offering. It doesn't technically need to be flowers (but flowers starts with F so it fits within this list). The gift might be food, candy, business equipment, or anything that the other party would enjoy receiving. It shouldn't just be a cheap gag gift that gets laughs. The intent is to offer something tangible that the other party sees as valuable. A valuable item demonstrates a genuine desire for fixing the collaborative relationship.

Creating common understanding can also be achieved through *feedback* with the opposition. Define a mutually agreeable mechanism to share reactions and perceptions over the wall of separation. "Do you agree that this is not working? Let's discuss how each of our sides is contributing to the problem." This exchange can be written or verbal; rigidly structured or open-ended; anonymous or with names attached; in breakout groups or one-on-one. Describe the harm that they do (disrupt, detract, deny, or destroy). The feedback should not be judgmental venting of the faults of the other party (e.g., "You're stupid" is not helpful). Rather, the feedback session should be managed as analytically as possible with a sense of ownership from both parties to solve their interaction difficulties. (One substrategy of *feedback* is to bring *facts* to the other side, to let them see data and gain empathy about the situation from the other perspective.) Ongoing feedback or follow-up is also necessary to demonstrate the continued resolve toward collaboration.

Fun (which is often "fyzical"/physical in nature) is a way to bring together two warring factions. Engage two groups outside of work in something that will promote laughter, which will in turn lower the defenses that were triggered by the UPT hostility. Shared fun/physical activities for the parties might include karaoke, golf, bowling, group dancing, tennis, team softball, rock climbing, etc. Avoid activities that could make some people uncomfortable due to age, infirmity, or cultural restrictions. The goal is to see people outside of their role as the "enemy" and instead see them for their shared values and commonalities. This sets the foundation for trust in the workplace.

Oppositional parties may be demonized, but it is much harder to propagate ill will if true *friendship* has been established. In a comfortable environment, such as a coffee hour, have the parties introduce themselves via personal rather than professional attributes. Hearing about nonwork details, such as families, hobbies, favorite music/movies, or nonprofessional aspirations can trigger a desire to see the other party be successful. This introduction process can be done as a group around a table or one-on-one in a social environment. Wherever such a gathering occurs, the success of this F tactic is highly dependent on the willingness and skills of both sides to *listen*, which is discussed in much greater detail in Chapter Nine.

If prolonged conflicts remain refractory to bridge-building efforts, bringing in a neutral party as a *facilitator* to intervene may be warranted. In this approach, two groups that have struggled to find trust engage a neutral third party to settle disputes. Typical third parties include leaders from another department, HR, or external emotional mediators. This is rarely looked upon as a pleasant approach, but in some cases it is the only effective mechanism to address persistent problems.

Lastly, if oppositional parties have not found improved ability to collaborate after other interventions, it may be necessary to limit extent of the interaction. Rather than having a broad list of outputs requiring collaboration, *focus* the relationship between the two parties through a more narrow definition. Limit the amount, frequency, and interfaces of interaction to minimize disruptive conflict. For example, if abrasive distrust occurs in every monthly meeting, create monthly written reports and hold meetings quarterly. Or, apply the decoupling techniques discussed earlier, leaving only a few items to be susceptible to human discussion. The *flight* tactic is not the same thing as *focus*; the former is a fear-rooted reflex to leave while the latter is an active choice to minimize interactions.

These seven Fs allow oppositional groups to potentially decrease their hostilities, or at least make progress in their ability to collaborate.

* * *

How Now

- *Assess the nine distrust symptoms (UPT) in your organization.* If earnings have been sluggish in your company, consider UPT as an explanation. Use the list of nine symptoms of distrust described in this chapter to do a rapid assessment within your organization. This assessment is best done in face-to-face interviews or focus groups. Members of senior management often conduct such discussions, but an external consultant can also facilitate these conversations.

- *Get over it.* If you have had a long-standing feud with someone in your company, it's time to end it. Use the social seven Fs to invite a connection with that person or that department today. You, the other party, and the company will be better for it.

- *Push for compromise.* If your organization cannot resolve a long-standing dispute, use the three tactics of grand exchange/mosaic/nuclear option to push for compromise.

Chapter Six:
Emotion as Business Strategy

The fourth emotional interface is connectedness to coworkers. This chapter describes how an enterprise brings together all its leaders and staff around a common emotional strategy as a basis for superlative performance.

Choices: the cover photo for the summer fashion catalog, the font of the restaurant menu, the lease terms on the headquarters offices in San Francisco, the vendor selection among bidders from Europe and Asia, the marketing plan for Brazil, the hostile takeover of a longtime competitor.

In business, choices are not fun shopping sprees for luxurious chocolates, cars, or cashmere. Business choices are urgent mandates among imperfect options. Some of the decisions are yes/no, while others are multiple choice (the really difficult kind from university exams, where there are answers like "a and c, but not b"). Every hour of every day, entrepreneurs and corporate managers must weigh the consequences of decisions of all sizes, from the nano to the giga.

Decisions are fraught with implications; each alternative might create blockbuster success or come back to haunt the enterprise. The karmic consequence of business decisions is that the actions of the past are never fully forgotten—eventually all the choices coalesce in the accounting income statement and balance sheet, the accumulated sum of layers of judgments and paths pursued.

The Business Choice of Emotion

Emotion is linked with a business from the day it begins. Start-ups and family-run ventures often originate in a stew of emotional worry; every initial investment carries inherent risk until things are up and running. For some small companies, problematic emotional dynamics derail them by surprise; eager entrepreneurs devote long hours of vigilance to operational, financial, creative, and management considerations but almost none to group culture and emotion. Over time, as organizations grow, uncertainties and pressures remain. Leaders worry about meeting payroll and paying off debt; frontline workers worry about job stability and workplace safety.

Despite this all-too-obvious association, companies have typically developed plans with little recognition of the impact of emotion. As noted in Chapter One, we would mock a corporation that says, "We avoid IT because it is messy," but we accept such assertions about emotion. On conference calls with shareholders and market analysts, companies offer precise details as varied as debt structures and new product packaging but have very few words to say about the emotional environment they embed within their walls to enable future earnings. This widespread avoidance may be rooted in a lack of corporate emotion frameworks and agreed-upon lexicon, but that is not a suitable justification going forward.

To correct the lack of attention on emotion, company boards and external stakeholders must expect senior management to provide such information. The board of directors reviews overall strategy on behalf of shareholders; they should include a discussion of emotional strategy in their expectations.

Lenders, market experts, and investment consultants should not only ask probing questions about revenue projections or operational efficiency to assess the soundness of a business, but also investigate the chosen emotional architecture that enables those revenues and efficiencies to be realized. Just as a savvy investment analyst will spot the problems of a business plan that includes overextended leverage or limited market presence, the same analyst will begin to point out undefined emotional strategy as a missing piece of a company's due diligence.

Group emotional strategy must be viewed as a rigorous company response to challenges internal and external to the business. Investments in the emotional environment must be made which ensure profitability of the enterprise for shareholders.

Creating Emotional Competitive Advantage

Long ago, companies realized the value of making decisions in advance of volatile market conditions. *Strategy is the aggregation of choices*, made in advance of circumstances, which guide the company's behavior and activities over a considerable duration of time (i.e., years) to optimize business results. What will allow us to be successful? Where are the risks and trade-offs?

Business strategy typically encompasses the choices related to products, finance, pricing, operations, technology, supply chain, innovation practices, product development pipeline, sales force, marketing, organizational structure, and talent management (there are dozens of additional issues that vary by industry). With the unifying intent of raising earnings and shareholder wealth, companies make informed decisions about what they will do versus what they will not do. Rivals in the same industry may make similar or differing decisions, forming their own competitive advantage.

The emotional strategy of a company is the sum of *choices of how we relate to others in the organization*. These choices collectively create competitive advantage. Humans feel together, but *how* they do so can be largely influenced by the decisions of the company.

Whether in small groups (such as a team) or in large entities (such as a company), humans are bonded by a similar set of emotional factors. Humans need sporadic doses of progress, peace, nurturance, inspiration, inclusion, imagination, gratitude, fun, and friendship to remain emotionally connected to each other for businesses to be successful. Thus, *the same nine emotions that unite a team are the emotional strategies that unite an entire business*, but the balance and implementation of them are quite different.

Within the confines of a team, all nine emotional needs must be met with a few small-scale actions. Within a business, it is impractical to try to deliver large-scale actions to meet all nine emotional needs for an entire organization; there just aren't enough resources to do so. Thus, the emotional strategy of a company identifies a subset of emotions that the company provides to everyone. Individual team members fill in the rest on a given team.

As an analogy, when a national government prioritizes a set of social services it can suitably provide as a safety net infrastructure, it is forced to leave the remainder of needs to the private sector and charities to deliver to vulnerable citizens. In the same way, a company decides which of the nine emotional needs it will support for all employees in the emotional strategy of the business, leaving the rest to individual employees and teams to provide for one another.

The infrastructure required to support an emotional strategy touches many elements of the talent management cycle for an organization: recruiting, orientation, capability building, leadership, performance evaluation, and compensation. Emotional strategy is not just another name for the HR processes, however; it encompasses specific tactics for how people sense connectedness to each other and how they collaborate to add value to the company. Companies should define their emotional strategy like a college student defines a field of study: "We're majoring in imagination, with a minor in progress."

Management teams can utilize different combinations of the nine strategies in unifying employees and building their sense of commonality toward a common purpose. Any combination of the nine strategies can work in any industry and in any business, large or small.

Not everyone will feel comfortable in every environment, though. Just as a job applicant may not desire to live in a particular geography, an individual job applicant will tend to gravitate to the emotional environments that make him or her most comfortable and professionally successful. This includes introverts and extroverts; a company can be emotionally connected in a variety of ways and still be a safe haven for those who prefer to work alone.

Emotional connectedness can, and should, include workers of all abilities and motivation levels. Managers must accept that their primary role is to foster a particular emotional environment to create value for the company; how a given worker fits into (and contributes to) that environment is a matter of day-to-day corrective guidance as well as periodic performance evaluation. Implementing an emotional strategy does *not* mean lowering expectations of employees or being more forgiving of unacceptable behavior; to the contrary, an emotional strategy provides a stronger rationale as to why some employees must not continue with the company. Those workers who detract from the ability of the company to create earnings should not stay.

I will review the nine strategies in forthcoming sections of this chapter, each beginning with an anecdotal view from of a hypothetical employee within a company (each character anecdote is for illustrative purposes only). For each strategy I also offer the definition of emotional connectedness (i.e., what makes employees think as "we" or "us"), implications for aesthetics and workplace design, unacceptable conduct, handling difficult transitions (e.g., terminations, workforce reductions, and cost reductions), and talent management protocols.

Emotional Strategy #1: Progress

Priscilla is a midlevel lab manager for a global pharmaceutical company. She has a traditional office, but she spends considerable time in laboratory spaces; she began her career fifteen years earlier as a lab scientist right out of graduate school. Her typical day includes meetings with her direct reports to assess accomplishments and upcoming resource needs. Priscilla documents progress of her teams in a software-based scorecard system, which senior leadership uses to understand the details of the business. Incentives have been generous for Priscilla, as her unit makes progress consistently; she knows the limits of compensation for those managers who don't deliver. She manages mostly based on timelines and deadlines. In the hallway of the company, high-definition video screens display daily news headlines from the corporate communications department, sharing the highlights of recent financial, operational, and scientific improvements made within the company. Priscilla loves progress.

*Emotional connectedness: Accomplishment and pride emotionally unite many esteemed groups, among them championship sports teams and premier academic institutions. The fulfillment of surpassing expectations binds people to others who want such results as well. Valiant effort actually results in something! The employees themselves must drive this though; the dictator boss who simply demands unreasonable output is not contributing to emotional connectedness or a healthy emotional strategy. Companies must recruit and develop people who would push for such results themselves without external pushing from management.

*Aesthetics/work space: Small reminders of accomplishments (e.g., photographs on hallway walls of completed projects, academic-style conference presentation boards) help to reinforce the ethos of achievement.

*Unacceptable conduct: There is little tolerance among peers for a coworker who doesn't try hard or takes too long to deliver, as he or she doesn't contribute to the progress of the organization.

*Handling cost reductions and workforce changes: Reductions in budgets or a downsizing workforce must be handled in accordance with all local laws and regulations, obviously, but in this strategy there is a strong need for formal communications to the organization. People need the reassurance that the current difficult circumstances (and the necessary cuts) do not diminish the progress of the company as a whole. Employees need to understand that the trajectory still remains hopeful for the organization and for them personally. For example, formal communications describing the past ebb and flow of costs or staffing (e.g., "We grew for eight straight years, scaled back for two, and then grew for eleven, and now we're scaling back at the moment") place current difficulties in a historical context of progress.

*Recruiting: Progress as an emotional strategy has two key implications for recruiting: selection of high achievers and promotion of internal stars. First, new candidates should be assessed for achievement orientation. Résumé achievements and extracurricular achievements will support this, as well as interviewing questions that focus on specific examples of high achievement (e.g., "Tell me about the most impact you've ever had"). Second, in this emotional strategy, executive jobs should almost always go to promoted internal candidates. There is pride in seeing a colleague advance through the company hierarchy; progress is about not only company results but also the progression of others. Seeing an outsider brought in for a leadership role will undermine such pride and internal cohesiveness of those who've come up through the system.

*Orientation/onboarding (orientation typically implies the transmission of key information for all employees, while onboarding represents the training and mentoring practices that make entry transitions smooth over the first few weeks): Progress is an emotional experience to share with new employees on the first day. For example, in addition to the standard review of benefits and employee manuals, have a manager review the scorecard for the company and have the new employees share in a brief celebration of the company's achievements. As well, identify a small deliverable/outcome within the company that the new employees (regardless of department) can complete together without supervision for a few hours *on orientation day*. Get something done. Such tasks might include organizing for an upcoming blood drive or nonconfidential clerical work that will support one of the departments to meet a deadline. The goal is to make people feel right away like contributors to achievements of the company.

*Capability building: Progress as an emotional strategy requires all employees, not just managers, to possess the key skill of time management; offer training in time management for new employees. While general training programs in functional and technical knowledge may be vital in some industries to maintain momentum, progress as an emotional strategy suggests a trade-off between long-term skills and the short-term pressure to keep things moving.

*Leadership/management: Companies that utilize progress as an emotional strategy "never met a scorecard they didn't like." Visual management displays communicate where things stand for all to see, and dashboards of red, yellow, and green lights are commonplace. These companies frequently utilize checklists. In some companies, share price is continuously transmitted on television screens in building lobbies so that everyone is aware of how the company is doing. The challenge for managers is to understand how to use progress as a *pleasant motivator* that employees desire rather than an overhanging threat that promotes fear. This includes the ability to listen and to avoid abusive terminology; the desire to progress provides sufficient pressure without additional manager threats to undermine enthusiasm.

*Performance evaluation: This emotional strategy removes the anxiety of semiannual reviews and replaces it with a steady stream of evaluation. There are no surprises, as everyone understands his or her own status continually. Staff should see the accomplishments of their group regularly highlighted in company communications to maintain the culture of progress. Use evaluation discussions to set future goals and targets, or provide corrective support for missed targets of the past. Termination decisions should be easy to document and determine (even if difficult emotionally to deliver), as performance data have been tracked since the employee joined the team.

*Compensation: In the progress emotional strategy, compensation should be neither a reason to stay nor a reason to leave. Achievement itself should be the motivator; bonuses based on overall company performance are desired.

Advancement to higher ranks of the echelon should be associated with meaningful increases in compensation.

Emotional Strategy #2: Peace

Peter is the vice president of claims in a multinational property insurance company. While the company provides him an office in a major urban skyscraper, he also spends significant time videoconferencing from home at unusual hours to interact with country managers across the globe. The company's dramatic growth history has mostly been through acquisition of regional insurers on multiple continents. More so than he expected, his promotion to VP brought with it the need to assuage cross-cultural misunderstandings. The claims function has been able to significantly reduce administrative costs under his leadership by a combination of centers of excellence with improved knowledge management. He describes his management style as "part shepherd, part ambassador" in working with very senior country managers. Overall, he feels he is a good fit for the company, as his bosses maintain a similarly calm demeanor and approach to minimizing friction internally.

*Emotional connectedness: Companies that use peace as an emotional strategy might be described as a "no-UPT zone." Peace is not a soft, new age, colleagues hugging, meditation with candles, vulnerable, dreamy form of work environment. Far from it. Peace as an emotional strategy implies a rigorous expectation of internal collaboration without internal sabotage or politics gone amok. Common to companies using peace as a strategy is use of respectfulness as a group norm and knowledge sharing. Codes of behavioral conduct ensure that threats come from outside the company, not within it.

*Aesthetics/work space: Visual images and artwork, such as photographs of company leaders standing together as a group, can subtly promote the sense of harmony in working spaces. "We get along."

*Unacceptable conduct: While all personality types can succeed in a company that adopts peace as an emotional strategy, individuals who possess a volatile temper will not be a good fit. Obviously, abrasive, impolite hooligans will undermine the ethos of peaceful coexistence.

*Handling cost reductions and workforce changes: Maintaining composure is difficult under normal circumstances but particularly challenging when people see budgets and colleagues diminishing. Within this strategy, leaders must proactively engage affected parties and find ways for people to adapt. Focusing on *shared* utilization of scarce technology, equipment, and resources will support peace.

*Recruiting: Initial interviewers might ask questions of potential candidates, like, "If a colleague embarrassed you in a meeting, how would you address the matter with him or her?" The answer aligned with this emotional strategy is to "gently approach him or her offline and discuss the concern." Avoidance ("I would just forget about it") is as bad an answer as an angry response, as the person who habitually suppresses his or her discomforts has the risk of "exploding" without warning. Experience with working in environments of diverse styles (cultures, ethnic origins, and talent levels) is a plus for hiring candidates into a company that adopts a peace strategy.

*Orientation/onboarding: If a company adopts peace as an emotional strategy, then listening skills training should be included in the initial orientation program (in the form described in Chapter Nine). Some organizations will discuss exact protocols for dispute resolution (of both behavioral and business decision matters) within onboarding to ensure that new employees follow them.

*Capability building: Training programs in companies using peace as an emotional strategy often serve two purposes: learning and bridge building. Rather than utilizing individual training approaches, such as online software for skill building, employees are brought together in a live training environment. Training allows the formation of basic acquaintances and friendships that will serve them in later parts of their careers. For example, when country managers Kimiko and Juanita are assigned to an international task force for a company restructuring initiative, they both reply, "Oh right, I remember I met her two years ago at the marketing training program in Zurich." Networks serve the broader goal of reducing UPT.

*Leadership/management: Listening is a basic requirement for all employees in a company adopting peace as an emotional strategy, but it is a core part of the job description for managers and executives. Without the ability to listen and utilize "Clinton-Mandela skills" (see Chapter Nine), managers will not be able to ameliorate internal hostilities that disrupt the success of the company. Managers or staff who engage in yelling, abusive language, harassment, humiliation, gossip, or other behaviors that create internal strife cannot be permitted to remain with the organization. Leaders in such companies are diplomats who minimize frictions among stakeholders with the *financial* intent of eliminating the "UPT earnings drainers"; they use trust to build treasure.

*Performance evaluation: Performance evaluations include a mix of traditional job metrics alongside an assessment of collaborative inclination. Combine supervisor reviews with 360-degree feedback around responsiveness and helpfulness to colleagues. Terminate abrasive employees even if they may be revenue rainmakers, as they detract from the ability of others in the company to be successful.

*Compensation: Compensation must support the idea of a "UPT-free zone" for this strategy. Formulas for compensation should be weighted more for overall company performance; reward people for working together for the company rather than their own interests.

Emotional Strategy #3: Nurturance

Nadia is the CEO of a multinational petrochemical company. Her career began as a field engineer in Russia thirty-five years earlier but subsequently included roles in three business units on six continents. Her entrepreneurial inclination was a good match for the people she worked with along the way. While being the first female leader of the company is notable, she is quick to note how vital her mentors Helmut, Jerome, Miguel, and Abdullah were in her progression. When she went through a painful divorce with two young children early in her career, Miguel invited her and her children to his family's home for dinner every Saturday. When she later moved to a position in the US headquarters, she was a mainstay in the company's superb dining center and coffee bar during many late hours, where she continued the tradition of mentoring young talent.

*Emotional connectedness: This is the strategy of all of animal life on the planet—the young are cared for in order for the species to survive. Wherever one looks in this kind of company, there are indicators that the leadership seeks to provide the resources needed for people to feel cared for, valued, and mentored. The company that adopts a nurturance emotional strategy believes that if people feel cared for, they will care about the business. Both peers and bosses informally provide emotional sustenance to cope with ongoing operational and organizational duties; colleagues frequently grab coffee together and discuss their challenges. People strive for success but not at the expense of those around them. "We take care of customers and each other" is their philosophy. It is important to distinguish nurturance versus peace. In a peace-driven environment (strategy 2), team members avoid and prevent harsh confrontation. In a nurturance-driven environment (strategy 3), harsh confrontation occurs at the normal frequency of any other business, but colleagues check on you afterward to make sure you're feeling okay about the interaction.

*Aesthetics/work space: Physical nourishment comes in the form of food, beverages, and exercise facilities. Emotional rejuvenation comes in the form of small, quiet rooms for individuals to remove themselves for a short period to decompress from stressful conditions. Group spaces have furniture, writing boards, and other materials for teaching and mentorship to occur.

*Unacceptable conduct: In this strategy, it's everyone's job to make sure the next generation of leaders are being groomed for the company's future, so mentorship is always a priority. Those persons who do not actively contribute to mentoring must receive corrective feedback as early as possible, and adapt their mind-set accordingly to contribute to the nurturance model.

*Handling cost reductions and workforce changes: This strategy will struggle the most with scaling back, as it is antithetical to the philosophy of investing in the future and making people cared for. To counteract the impact of such reductions on the business, leaders should focus on *professional staff development opportunities* in the new environment. For example, the leadership should explain in detail how the reductions affect mentoring, advancement, new roles for people to take on, and the future of the business.

*Recruiting: The company that applies nurturance as its emotional strategy must seek people who are willing to be mentored and who are willing to mentor others. Volunteering experience with charitable organizations is one way to identify such individuals. There is a strong emphasis on building senior talent rather than hiring it from the outside, as mentorship is expected of leaders.

*Orientation/onboarding: New employees at a company whose emotional strategy is nurturance will feel immediately welcomed and cared for. Executive leaders will make an appearance at all orientation days and personally invite questions from the audience. Managers will invite new employees to a small group lunch in order to cultivate mentoring relationships as part of onboarding. In some organizations, employees will be assigned a supervisor who manages/evaluates their performance versus a separate nonevaluative mentor who coaches and provides a reassuring voice of experience.

*Capability building: The philosophy of this strategy is that ensuring employee well-being and professional development is the best way to ensure business results. Senior staff highlight role modeling and mentoring in this emotional strategy over traditional training programs. Such companies take great pride in stating, "We build great leaders here," using a variety of means to accomplish that outcome.

*Leadership/management: Leaders and managers in a nurturance-driven company are counselors and coaches. Managers must be aware of the emotional signals of those they supervise. With those colleagues who appear overwhelmed or withdrawn, the leader must support them (e.g., like Miguel did for Nadia) through difficult periods. This includes providing emotional nourishment, such as unsolicited compliments. There must be an expectation to consistently invest their time in mentoring.

*Performance evaluation: Followership is a key element of performance reviews. Central to understanding which employees are creating the desired working environment are 360-degree feedback mechanisms.

*Compensation: Individual compensation becomes less of a concern in this emotional strategy, as group needs weigh more heavily. Earnings are reinvested into quality of life for all workers through better working space, premium food and beverages, workout facilities, spaces for rejuvenation (quiet rooms, balconies/verandas), onsite child care, onsite health care, and concierge perks (e.g., dry cleaning).

Emotional Strategy #4: Inspiration

Ignacio is a junior loan officer in a bank branch that caters to small businesses and local companies. He has been with the bank for just over two years. Since the time he joined, he has been involved in the company's community volunteer program. He helped take toys to the children's hospital, did beach cleanup, and is currently the co-organizer of the upcoming blood drive. He gets animated about putting on identical T-shirts with fifty other bank employees at such events. Company leaders not only aspire to have notable impact in the community, but also believe that such involvement supports the brand and the company's growth. "We can do anything" is the refrain of leaders who wish to bring an uplifting tone to company volunteerism as well as motivating employees to reach stretch targets.

*Emotional connectedness: Those involved in social movements are often swept up in a wave of emotional intensity. Even when business actions are executed in the ambition of increasing earnings, emotional belief in the greater good or a noble purpose is a powerful way to keep stakeholders engaged within the company. Volunteers and benefactors often talk about the "high" or "magical feeling" associated with doing acts of charity.

*Aesthetics/work space: The working environment in a company using inspiration as an emotional strategy contains motivational landscape photographs with captioned themes, such as a view from a mountaintop with the word "pinnacle" underneath. Faith-based organizations, such as hospitals or charities, may include symbols/sculptures of their religion or framed quotations from sacred texts in conference rooms.

*Unacceptable conduct: Selfishness is frowned upon in an inspiration-led environment. Though the business requires earnings to exist, in this environment sales are viewed as tools of meeting the mission. The company exists to have lasting impact in the world, not only to make money. Behavior that puts self-interest above company or community is viewed as improper.

*Handling cost reductions and workforce changes: In the inspiration-led company, changes to budgets and workforce must be positioned entirely vis-à-vis the mission. Explain to the organization why various reductions were short-term necessities toward the long-term vision. If the actions help meet the mission, then the organization is more likely to rebound quickly.

*Recruiting: Attracting individuals of high caliber is done through emphasis on the impact of one's work. Design interview questions to assess ability to inspire and be inspired, such as "How did your most significant personal achievement lead to benefit for others?"

*Orientation/onboarding: Inspiration can begin on day one with stories and data about the work of the company, both in its impressive scale (e.g., "Our buses transport two hundred thousand children to school every day") and its impact (e.g., "Our employees logged ten thousand volunteer hours last year"). Within this strategy, new employees must see themselves as more than just employees: they are noble individuals doing something of great importance.

*Capability building: If a training program is positioned as an element of a road map to a future state, then it has the potential to inspire. If not, then it will be viewed as irrelevant. Coaching and mentoring generally have a greater potential to inspire than formal lectures.

*Leadership/management: Inspirational leadership can take a wide range of forms, from the servant leader model to the eloquent orator. Corporate leaders may inspire others by talking about their hopes for the company, their own commitment to improving the community, or the impact the company has on society and the world. The management group must serve as role models if inspiration is the chosen emotional strategy, as an uninspiring leadership team will be ineffective at generating emotional connectedness.

*Performance evaluation: Inspirational activity can be measured via a subjective component from peers within a 360-degree evaluation (e.g., "How does this employee make those around him or her better?") or an explicit recognition of extramural activities (e.g., performance evaluation credit for involvement in charitable organizations).

*Compensation: Inspiration as an emotional strategy does not specifically suggest compensation should be handled in a specific manner. Some companies choose to reward employees financially for inspirational activity, while other firms choose to redirect some portion of earnings toward charitable causes.

Emotional Strategy #5: Inclusion

Inga is a junior technical artist for the video game division of an international entertainment company. She looks at graphic art sketches and listens to vague preliminary notions of game developers, and then writes computer code to make them into prototype characters and visual settings. Following a string of major flops at the company, new leaders have introduced a major shift in how the company designs games. Rather than a cabal of young men making all the creative decisions, a broader group of employees are now involved in the early stages of game development. Where Inga once sat silently in creative meetings, taking notes as an anonymous observer, she now has the ability to say what she thinks in meetings as a contributor. Several recent projects have taken dramatic turns in early stage development as a result of the broader input approach. Company leaders are excited by early buzz on their upcoming releases that have a different flair, which they internally attribute to the new "speak up" culture.

*Emotional connectedness: Inclusion strategy utilizes the universal need for belonging. In this strategy, people are able to share their thoughts and ideas in order to feel that sense of belonging. Even when someone expresses an idea that sits outside the norm of the group's thinking, they give it due respect and fully hear it. Everyone is allowed to give an idea its public moment, because everyone accepts the egalitarian nature of perspective sharing. Inclusion is a useful business strategy because it minimizes the possibility of unforeseen risks or change inertia; if all ideas are openly presented, then the company has a better grasp of what challenges they must address. (Inclusion as an emotional strategy should not be confused with inclusiveness, which generally connotes actions for broadening employee ethnic diversity.)

*Aesthetics/work space: The steady stream of conversations occurring in these companies makes finding a quiet hallway a rare experience. People are frequently knocking on their boss's door to bring up an issue that they need to resolve. The physical environment matches the "speak up" culture with flyers/notice boards next to coffee areas, large group spaces where town hall meetings can comfortably occur, and corporate poster case examples of frontline worker ideas that have improved earnings ("speak-up superstars").

*Unacceptable conduct: Dismissing an idea before it is fully heard is the primary sin in these environments. There is not necessarily peace or nurturance, though; having the ability to share perspectives does not mean that people are utilizing diplomacy in their reactions or mentoring on how to be a more effective speaker.

*Handling cost reductions and workforce changes: When difficult changes are required, the inclusion-driven organization uses a committee approach to make such determinations. Individual leaders should not make such large-scale cost-cutting decisions arbitrarily, as that is contrary to the philosophy of bringing others into the discussion.

*Recruiting: Inclusion is a business ethos that upholds the right for everyone and every idea to be included in the decision-making process. Recruiting individuals who will fit with such a company strategy requires asking about comfort with consideration of alternative points of view; an interview question might be, "Name a decision that you made once, describe the options you faced, and give a convincing argument about why other options could have been correct."

*Orientation/onboarding: Speak Up! There could be a banner hanging up in the orientation room for the new employees with these two words. From day one, it must be clear that the only failure in this kind of company is to withhold a blockbuster growth idea or a wise warning of an upcoming danger. Withholding either will threaten earnings. The new employees must also be informed that mocking another person's idea is unacceptable.

*Capability building: Public speaking is a critical skill for all staff in an inclusion emotional strategy, as they must have comfort in providing a contrarian view. Confidence supports the ability to speak truth to power. Without this skill the strategy fails. Offer training programs, as necessary, to support the public speaking skill set.

*Leadership/management: Leaders and managers play three atypical roles in a company that uses inclusion as an emotional strategy: convener, listener, and opportunity finder. First, managers pull people together to decide, not decide for the people. Second, management must be skilled in the art of different forms of listening (see Chapter Nine). Third, leaders must look for opportunities for each employee to take on important responsibilities. The environment is truly inclusive only if everyone gets at least one chance to shine and be the hero.

*Performance evaluation: Evaluation should reflect whether the employee speaks up when needed to contribute to the success of the company.

*Compensation: People will perceive disproportionate bonus structures that allow only a few to reap financial rewards as antithetical to the inclusion strategy.

Emotional Strategy #6: Imagination

Imogene is the CEO of a nonprofit charity focused on creating business opportunities in impoverished urban areas in the United States. Possessing three graduate degrees, she has written two books on wealth disparities and testified before governmental leaders. Her hard-edged style strikes some as relentless, but she is consistently able to draw in donations when other charities are struggling. She utilized social networking sites to expand her donor database before it was a fad, and she has held numerous provocative fund-raising events that go against the conventional wisdom of the social sector. She is relentless with details for each new donor initiative. Her behind-the-scenes profanity is legendary, as are her late-night conference calls with her "idea team" with whom she kicks around ideas while sitting in her pajamas. Every staff member contributes ideas on a regular basis, and at least once a month they do brainstorming with no constraints on the ideas. People have fun in her organization by thinking up inventive ways to do ordinary things.

*Emotional connectedness: The imagination emotional strategy connects people through dreaming together and bringing the wow factor to each other (in addition to customers). Emotional connectedness comes through the act of contributing small pieces to a big answer. Since the brain is the source of both creative cognition and congregational connectedness, big ideas generate big emotion!

*Aesthetics/work space: An imagination-focused environment is typically nontraditional in order to stimulate extraordinary creativity. Furniture, decoration, use of space, color schemes, music, and availability of play areas are all part of the scheme.

*Unacceptable conduct: Individuals who do not venture outside their intellectual comfort zone will not be a good fit in these environments. The organization thrives on trying new things, even if they fail. Mistakes and failures are viewed as lessons. The only failure is not to try.

*Handling cost reductions and workforce changes: In organizations following this strategy, difficult cost reduction choices will trigger numerous alternative proposals (e.g., "But what if we cut down on the use of paper clips instead?"). Allowing employees to suggest new ways to maintain momentum (e.g., an idea contest) in the new environment will channel such creativity and reengage those who feel discouraged by tough circumstances.

*Recruiting: Companies that adopt imagination as an emotional strategy are looking for individuals who commit themselves to solving big problems and are inherently happy with the opportunity to work on big issues. Since such answers don't come during normal business hours when someone is sitting at a desk, the best candidates will be those who feel comfortable running with an idea whenever it comes up. Puzzles that test ingenuity can be a useful screening tool in initial candidate assessment.

*Orientation/onboarding: During orientation, include a group activity that promotes creative problem solving. This might be a group construction task (e.g., building a durable bridge at least four feet long using only dental floss and duct tape), a group insight task on which to align (e.g., counting the number of rectangles within a complex painting), or a cooperative knowledge task (e.g., giving each person two clues to a mystery that the group must solve together within twenty minutes).

*Capability building: The same tasks/games used in orientation can be applied in training programs as well to stimulate innovative inclination along with whatever content is the focus of the training. The goal is to consistently match new capabilities with the clever problem solving they are intended to promote.

*Leadership/management: Managers should keep the focus of the organization on solving problems together. Keep people focused on the joy of doing the impossible together.

*Performance evaluation: Traditional metrics are less relevant in this strategy. Examples of preferred attributes for frontline and executive evaluations are: ability to apply frameworks across disciplines, ability to see complex patterns within chaos, flexibility in deploying oneself and others to solve issues as they arise, and disaggregates large ambiguities into manageable challenges.

*Compensation: Big ideas generate big emotion, but they should also generate big bonuses. Those within a company adopting an imagination strategy understand the need for stimulating revolution through reward stimulation.

Emotional Strategy #7: Gratitude

Graham is a young salesman in the family lumber company founded by his great-grandfather. Four generations of his ancestors have invested their lives in growing the business.

Today it is a healthy company with an excellent outlook. Hanging in the lobby of the main office are photographs from 1910 of Graham's great-grandfather, who came to Nebraska with his cousins and began the business with only a few dollars in their pockets. Now, the store closes every year on October 10, and the company invites all prior employees (they call themselves "alumni") back on that day to join in a festive meal, reminisce, and tell stories. The elderly alumni tell funny stories about Graham's ancestors. They become overwhelmed, thinking about how much they gained by being a part of the store. They always end the annual gathering with a toast; they all stand and raise a wine glass and say in unison, "Thank you. I was here and you helped me." The same spirit of gratitude exists between the company and its customers; each December the company sends out gifts of appreciation to the most loyal customers.

*Emotional connectedness: The expression of gratitude is a strong uniting force, as it acknowledges respect and emotional linkage. In an organization where gratitude is the emotional strategy, people appreciate the acts of each other and feel they owe something to the past. Appreciation has two meanings: to say thanks and to increase in value. Expressions of gratitude do both for the receiver.

*Aesthetics/work space: At a subtle level, gratitude is manifested through visual recognition of legacy (e.g., pictures of founders on walls). In companies applying this strategy, frontline workers often save small notes of appreciation and place them in lockers, on desks, or in the plastic pouch behind their ID badge.

*Unacceptable conduct: When someone reaches a milestone or accomplishes a goal, it is expected that people humbly recognize the efforts of others who helped that person. The "I earned this myself" attitude is unacceptable in this strategy.

*Handling cost reductions and workforce changes: Separations and reductions can be agonizing, but they should still offer moments for colleagues to express gratitude in written and oral forms. People will want the chance to say thanks to each other before they depart. This strategy promotes the unusual circumstance where former employees are likely to maintain some collegiality after they are downsized.

*Recruiting: Gratitude-focused companies are dependent on having savvy business individuals who are humbly able to acknowledge others. Whether in sales, order fulfillment, or post-sale customer relationship management, this strategy requires individuals who demonstrate polite language and courtesy (e.g., "please," "thank you," "you're welcome").

*Orientation/onboarding: Gratitude can be integrated into an orientation session by providing each new employee a blank card and asking him or her to write a note of appreciation to someone who helped him or her to secure his or her new job (e.g., the friend who encouraged the employee to apply or the interviewer with whom he or she really connected).

*Capability building: Training programs should embody appreciative behaviors, such as having each participant shake hands with the trainer/speaker afterward to personally thank that person for his or her lessons.

*Leadership/management: Frontline employees will not demonstrate the gratitude model with customers and colleagues if their supervisors do not also do it. Leaders must carry forth a mind-set of "To whom do I owe my success?" and offer appreciation accordingly. This should be in a mix of forms, including written notes, gifts such as fruit baskets, quiet appreciative comments, and public recognition. There is a strong risk of backfire if a manager's appreciation sounds rehearsed or if it feels inauthentic; recipients know a scam when they hear it.

*Performance evaluation: Alter terminology in reviews to fit with this strategy. For example, rather than referring to positive performance as strengths, refer to such evidence in a review session instead as "appreciated contributions to the business."

*Compensation: In companies where people feel that their contributions are emotionally valued, bonuses are less of a motivator. Income is not the primary driver that keeps staff and executives enthusiastic to remain part of the company. Disproportionate or unfair distribution of bonuses will make everyone else feel undervalued, however.

Emotional Strategy #8: Fun

Fujiko is the forty-three-year-old head of IT for a midsize paper goods and office supply company in East Asia. Her company has historically been a home for hardworking, serious people who prefer steadiness, structured routine, and serenity. Now, the management team has adopted a startling new attitude in the wake of six consecutive quarters of business losses: fun. The leadership team analyzed market research/customer feedback data to pinpoint their business problem, and it is the morale of the staff. Two large customers switched their accounts to a rival company, offering comments, including "It's a gloomy place representing old ways" and "Your sales staff are chronically unhappy." In looking at options for reenergizing the sales force and internal staff, the leaders now encourage people to be joyous as they approach their work. Fujiko has always been a bit unconventional, wearing brightly colored eyeglass frames and equally vivid shoes; she now feels free to express her playful nature in the workplace. She has encouraged her small

IT team to decorate their work spaces with toys and dolls, a trend that has spread all the way to the executive offices (the CEO has a little robot dog that barks and walks around in the corner of his office). The purchasing division is having a video game tournament at lunch on Friday. The marketing team is capitalizing on the internal culture in its new advertisements, which include photographs of laughing employees, like Fujiko. "It may seem strange to be this excited about toner cartridges and staplers, but around here, we are."

*Emotional connectedness: People work in greater alignment with those who make it fun to be around them. Having fun is not necessarily counterproductive, as many leaders fear; playfulness is the antidote to anxiety, stress, and UPT inherent to many workplaces. A playful attitude can *enhance* a rigorous work ethic. Each person's daily routine is impacted by the connectedness to others, as duties become more efficient when done in the highest spirit of collaboration.

*Aesthetics/work space: Changing the working space can support the convergence of work with emotional enjoyment. Walking into the hallway of a business that utilizes fun as an emotional strategy can be a surreal experience: Hawaiian-style decorations, skateboarding arcs in the hallway, laughter, video game devices next to the coffee machines. Desks are decorated at the discretion of each worker and might include toys, photos, action figures, funny posters, souvenirs from recent office parties, or artwork.

*Unacceptable conduct: Workers frown upon those colleagues who abstain consistently from the group's enjoyment. Those who criticize laughter, or perceive humor as frivolous, will be a poor fit.

*Handling cost reductions and workforce changes: Treat sad news, such as budget constraints and downsizing, with appropriate sobriety, and don't make it into something fun. The way to maintain the emotional strategy for remaining workers is to temporarily suspend fun activities or frolicking (e.g., for two weeks) until the group feels ready to return to the normal pace.

*Recruiting: It only takes one curmudgeon as the "party pooper" to ruin the fun for others. Interviewing must focus on goodness of fit.

*Orientation/onboarding: Most people have not simultaneously learned and played since kindergarten. The process of bringing people into such an environment may involve reshaping fundamental attitudes about the nature of work and the basis of business success. Thus, extend orientation schedules to include training on how to work in such an environment. Assessing goodness of fit is difficult to do through traditional interviewing; short-term probationary periods (e.g., three weeks) allow for a much better assessment of whether one can fit into such an environment. As well, it may be necessary to have people depart from the organization early in the process if it is clearly not a good fit.

*Capability building: Link learning with playing to stay consistent with the emotional strategy. Avoid traditional didactic seminars.

*Leadership/management: The job of leaders in a fun strategy is to set targets, provide strategic trajectory, ensure the right emotional ethos, and then get out of the way to allow joy to link people together. The supervisor does not need to micromanage fun. It may be difficult to bring in traditional managerial talent from other environments if they are unwilling to embrace enjoyment.

*Performance evaluation: Many individuals who are productive in a traditional environment may struggle in a fun workplace. Yet, the right worker here is actually *more* productive. For example, consider a traditional unenthusiastic environment, where each worker moderately produces 1.5 widgets per hour for 8 entire hours, or 1.5 x 8 = 12 widgets per shift. Then, compare such performance to a fun workplace, where each worker joyously produces 2 widgets per hour for only 7 hours (as one hour is devoted to fun/relaxation/laughter), 2.0 x 7 = 14. In the fun environment, the pace remains high for more productivity. Customer service and customer relationship metrics also reflect the impact of fun; the happier the employees, the more likely they are to be empathetic, enthusiastic, and effective at meeting customer needs.

*Compensation: Workers in fun environments typically view compensation as one of the lesser factors that correlate to their overall job satisfaction. The goal is to have an adequately high salary base that people don't distrust the fun environment as a gimmick substitute for basic needs.

Emotional Strategy #9: Friendship

Frank is a new junior analyst in the internal strategy group of a major specialty chemicals manufacturer. His job involves sitting in a small cubicle and combing through large volumes of scientific and financial data in isolation, along with producing short documents to review with his boss. Frank has always been an introvert and prefers work that he can do independently. He has always worked around other aloof, unemotional types as a matter of choice. Now, a recent tragedy in his workplace has changed everything for the company: a disgruntled former employee in one of the production plants brought a rifle into the workplace two months ago and killed fourteen workers before turning the weapon on himself. The leadership of the company immediately stopped production in all plants for one week to bring together the organization; mediators and counselors helped people to talk about what happened. In the process, people spoke about their own stresses. Since work has resumed, many colleagues remain introverted in cubicles but are spending more time with colleagues outside of work. Managers are inviting their team members to play golf; a few folks from operations have organized a social event calendar of museum trips, movies, and sports matches so that no one has to feel alone on the weekend. Frank never expected to be friends with people at work, but he increasingly sees where such connections have helped him to do his *job* better. He faces very little resistance from internal stakeholders when asking for their data or buy-in to an improvement initiative, as many of the same people play football with him on Thursday evenings. The executive team wants to maintain the friendship networks, as they have observed a dramatic improvement in operational metrics.

*Emotional connectedness: Work together by day, and go bowling together at night. The friendship emotional strategy views a seamless relationship between coworkers that implies connectedness in whatever setting they need such support. The friendship strategy is very different from nurturance or fun; in those other environments, people support each other in whatever ways they need *at work,* but such support does not necessarily extend *beyond* the workplace. Friendship creates business success through an elimination of UPT.

*Aesthetics/work space: The friendship-driven environment contains prominent announcements of social events, as well as welcome/introduction boards that have new employee names next to photos. Selected rooms should have furniture that supports people sitting together, such as sofas for multiple people in lounge areas rather than individual chairs.

*Unacceptable conduct: This strategy requires coworkers to engage with others to a significant degree; introverts can find less intensive ways to participate but should not exclude themselves entirely.

*Handling cost reductions and workforce changes: The key to managing difficult transitions in this strategy is to ensure that employees can choose to maintain their relationships even if colleagues are forced to work elsewhere because of financial constraints. Creating an alumni database of former colleagues on an ongoing basis helps to ensure this.

*Recruiting: The expectations of what workers in the friendship strategy environment do together must be part of the up-front interviewing process, such that candidates can self-select out of the process if such an environment makes them uncomfortable. Similarly, recruitment should include an arm of social cultivation for top talent, such as an invitation to a manager's home for a meal to discuss questions.

*Orientation/onboarding: Build social friendships early, starting at orientation. Have people wear large name tags, include an icebreaker activity that forces new hires to engage with each other to learn more about their nonwork identities (e.g., favorite movies, pets, hobbies). Alongside discussions of protocols and benefits, HR staff should describe the role of friendship networks in company functioning.

*Capability building: Like with the peace strategy, training programs are an opportunity to form friendships with colleagues. They should be conducted in person rather than online, with adequate time for socializing before or after the training event.

*Leadership/management: Leaders in the friendship strategy must be aware of which employees are withdrawn or disengaged in order to gently suggest ways to bring them into the broader community (without coming across like a cult). The job of the manager is to ensure that each worker feels connected to at least one other person so that there are no "friendless islands" in the company.

*Performance evaluation: Like with the peace or nurturance strategies, individuals who are abrasive will detract from the effectiveness of the strategy. Such individuals must receive corrective guidance.

*Compensation: As with several other emotional strategies, compensation is a lower priority compared with the social connection they gain from employment. Unfair or disproportionate compensation can undermine the sense of connectedness.

Here is a quick mnemonic for those who wish to retain these nine strategies for future reference: If it is difficult to remember the names of the nine categories, try remembering the names/stories of the nine fictional characters. Each of their names starts with the same letter as the name of the strategy.

Priscilla loves progress.
Peter promotes peace.
Nadia needs nurturance.
Ignacio desires inspiration.
Inga welcomes inclusion.
Imogene craves imagination.

Graham appreciates gratitude.
Fujiko fosters fun.
Frank finds friendship.

The Inevitable Difficult Period

Commercial ventures always have a potential downside; both leaders and workers alike must recognize that prosperity is never guaranteed. Business exists to generate earnings for those who take risk; it does not exist purely to provide financial security for executives or workers who devote their time. There will always be the possibility of going through a difficult period where a company struggles.

Some leaders will resist the entire concept of an emotional connectedness strategy out of apprehension for the inevitable day when leaders deliver bad news (e.g., individual terminations for poor performance, plant closures for cost reductions, postmerger workforce reductions). The thinking goes, "I don't want to care about others and be nice to them because someday I might have to fire them." Emotional connectedness, at first glance, feels irreconcilable with severe business decisions based on financial factors. This prompts some individuals to remain distant from the people they supervise.

To address this hesitation, managers must come to view emotional connectedness as a *necessary investment* in conducting business in the modern environment. Companies and individual leaders always hesitate about expenditures for IT, training, employee health coverage, office furniture, and so on. Nonetheless, executives understand that such investments are necessary to maintain the company's ability to compete in a competitive marketplace. It is the cost of doing business. Emotional connectedness is another such necessity in the modern economy, given team-based value creation and the need to reduce oppositional stakeholder tensions.

Consider if we apply the same irrational apprehension to the rest of life: "I will not care about my wife because someday I may need to divorce her." "I will not love my parents because someday I will need to bury them." "I will not adore my children because someday they will leave for college." One can exist in a state of constant avoidance of future pain and become minimally attached to everything as a result (sadly we all know some isolated people who actually do function in this manner). But is a minimal commitment to family really a family? Is a minimal connection to life really a life?

Is a business composed of minimally connected colleagues (generating minimal earnings together) really a business?

The important lesson for companies as they execute their emotional strategies is to have clarity in the relationship between the company and the workers from the beginning. For each of the emotional strategies, the onboarding message must include the reality that "the employment relationship must end for all of us at some point." Both sides must realize that the option for employer and employee to end the emotional connection is bought with the price of separation risk. Either side can walk away if it needs to, but hopefully it will never come to that point. Employees are free to leave for better opportunities even if it hurts the company badly, and companies must have the agility to adjust to shifting market demands.

To the degree that employees walk in with expectations of a lifelong social contract, the business must directly address agreement versus departure from that expectation. Clarification of what the emotional relationship will look like must begin early, perhaps with new employees in orientation sessions or even the recruiting process. Would one enter a lifelong marriage without discussing specific expectations for children, money, or religion? Just as some couples choose to enter premarital counseling to explore issues prior to making a more lasting commitment, businesses and potential employees must understand the risks they take and emotional connection they require to make it work for both sides. The emotional agreement between an employer and a new employee must be transparent (and not implied) from the day the employee enters the front door.

Implementation Errors of Emotional Strategy

There are four errors common to implementing a new emotional strategy:

1. Starting strong and then fading
2. Trying to keep everyone happy
3. Doing the superficial but not the serious
4. Being inconsistent

The first "wrong" way to implement an emotional strategy is to give it initial excitement but then fail to maintain momentum during stressful crunch periods or downturns. It cannot be a flavor-of-the-month initiative with just an occasional mention in the unread company newsletter. The strategy should be a compass for the daily activities of the company in good times and bad; otherwise, it is simply an internal gimmick to abandon at the first sign of trouble.

The second misstep of emotional strategy execution is the attempt to do all nine to keep everyone happy. Invariably, doing all nine strategies simultaneously translates to inadequate resources put against each of the tactics. They each fail to reach minimum threshold levels, such that UPT continues and earnings are depleted. Once a company defines its short list of emotional priorities (e.g., no more than three), the company must fully let go of the other strategies. Individual small working *teams* within the company should ensure they meet all nine needs (as discussed in Chapter Four), but the *company* should not make large investments or enact protocols in all nine. It dilutes the effectiveness and clarity of the chosen strategy.

The third path to failure is to do easy superficial tactics without also adopting the more serious ones. For example, it might be enticing to promote the idea of nurturance as a strategy, but it fails if leaders are not held accountable for sufficient mentoring in performance reviews, or upgrade investments are not made to the office space, including comfort foods and quiet spaces.

The last way for emotional strategy to fail is to choose a strategy that runs counter to the remainder of the company's strategic choices in customer experience, operations, marketing, finance, IT, or organizational structure. There needs to be a fit between emotional strategy and the rest of these strategies. Different actions of a company must also be consistent; if the overall emotional strategy is progress, then the HR team should not be promoting friendship at orientation and emphasizing imagination during performance reviews.

Choosing an Emotional Strategy for You

To conclude the discussion of emotional strategy on an inspirational note, imagine yourself in the following dreamlike situation: You arrive very early for the first day of work at a new position. You have not been told much about the company, your job description, or whom you'll be working with. You park your car in the otherwise empty lot and walk into the front lobby. The building appears empty. You are pleased with the furnishings and aesthetics of the space.

As you look upward, there is an enormous banner hung along the ceiling of the lobby atrium. You meditate on the simplicity of the large empty canvas; it appears unfinished. Then, letters slowly appear, as if invisible paint is gradually coming into view. The banner now simply has one word printed in capital letters. You take a deep breath and read the word, and it instantly brings you joy and comfort. You smile brightly, knowing that you are in exactly the right place for you.

What is that word?

Your answer is the emotional strategy in which you should work, the company type that will bring you fulfillment and emotional connectedness to others. (Hopefully the word for you is not "sleep," "doughnuts," or something inappropriate for children to hear!) You will bring your best to such a company and reap the greatest rewards as a result.

* * *

How Now

- *The board of directors should expect an emotional strategy summary from the CEO.* Hold the senior management accountable for the impact of social neuroscience on earnings. Demand a formal CEO presentation to the board on matters of emotional connectedness as a basis for customer growth, minimizing internal frictional losses, and organizational development.

- *Investors and analysts should expect an emotional strategy summary from an entrepreneur or company.* In order to make a sound investment decision, assess the risks. This includes determining whether a company (large or small) has done its homework in regard to how emotional catastrophe is being prevented and how emotional connectedness is being managed.

- *Leaders should integrate an emotional strategy component into existing strategic planning.* As organizations discuss the challenges and opportunities on the horizon within the strategic planning process, include an emotional component. You can do this with the traditional structure of a steering committee, with working groups examining various emotional strategy tactics and required changes to protocols and necessary investments.

- *Select managers carefully.* Select managers with great care, and avoid the historical forces for promotion. Rather than making promotion a reward for performance or seniority or making the boss look good, potential managers must be identified for their behavioral capacity to implement a particular emotional strategy and supported with the appropriate training, coaching, and mentoring in how to lead others.

Chapter Seven:
It's Really Bad around Here

This chapter does not pertain to everyone or every business. If you and your colleagues feel pain in the workplace, this chapter is for you. There are selected environments where a vacuum of emotion fills with toxic forces. When punishment or greed infects a company, it slowly destroys emotional connectedness. The downward spiral that ensues can lead to the end of a business. Yet, there are countermeasures to fix a badly broken situation.

The previous four chapters provide a comprehensive set of emotional tactics for a company to flourish in the modern marketplace, where services and collaboration play a vital role. However, there are some businesses where such tactics are *unlikely* to provide significant benefit because destructive emotions are already entrenched within the organization.

Every day across the planet, untold millions of people go to work in a place they dread. Their organizations are slowly dying, not from the burdens of fickle financial markets or declining product popularity but from the systematic suppression of emotional connectedness. Businesses and national economies cannot survive without basic trust among people, but in some entities trust is all but gone. It is only a matter of time before the business is gone as well.

As employees arrive each morning in these companies, their internal organs transmit to them an unpleasant visceral warning. They begin to experience a mix of nausea, anxiety, anger, disappointment, and fatigue before they even arrive in the parking lot. Both entry-level and executive staff members know that they walk into an oncoming extraction of their emotional reserves. Through individual resilience and honoring commitments to others (e.g., providing income for their family) they return each day to work, but eventually they will be completely drained.

Within their working day, employees in these environments encounter frequent dismissal of their ideas, intimidation and public humiliation from supervisors, chaotic changes to project scope and direction, uncomfortable unpredictability of their working hours, and unwarranted criticism of their labor in spite of diligent effort. The frontline clerical assistant, midlevel manager, and corporate executive all encounter a similar cacophony of hurtful assaults on their identity and sense of productivity.

In these environments, employees begin to feel dehumanized; the intrinsic emotional tendencies of their brain are chronically repudiated. None of the nine emotional strategies is in place, which fosters the dehumanization of workers within the organization. Such devastation can afflict even the most altruistic and service-oriented settings. Physicians in such a hospital may come across as devoid of empathy, teachers in such a school may appear annoyed by children, and clergy in such a parish might display indifference in the face of suffering. Such attitudes may appear to observers as individual employee traits, but they are often a reflection of intense organizational pain.

This anguish does not stay secret. Customers and business partners can easily identify such environments. One employee actually yells at the customers, another evokes guilt in the customers for bothering the employee, and another offers the absolute minimum effort required to complete a transaction. It may sound ridiculous to suggest that a customer could walk into a retail store and be punched in the face by an employee, but in some environments such wild scenarios are not that big a leap from reality.

Are you in one of these companies?

If this description sounds entirely implausible or you have not witnessed such issues in your business career, then congratulations—you are in the fortunate majority, where such emotionally toxic patterns will not threaten you or your company.

If you've read this chapter with a sense of familiarity, then you are not alone. Vast numbers of people in your company feel the same way you do, even though no one openly discusses it or makes things better. If you have begun to believe that enduring the bad situation is your only option, then this chapter is meant for you. But first, it is important to understand *why* an emotionally destructive environment develops as a prerequisite to understanding *what you can do* to make things better.

An Emotional Vacuum Invites Disaster

Emotionally *destructive* environments almost always begin as emotionally *disconnected* environments.

A company's descent typically follows a gradual sequence:

1. Disconnected/absent emotional strategy
2. Disruptive event occurs (minor or major)
3. Entrance of behavioral "F responses"
4. Greed and punishment strategies enhanced
5. Emotional destruction ends in business failure

The human species has always depended on emotional connectedness as a means of survival, as noted in multiple previous chapters. In the absence of such attachment, humans deteriorate. Isolation is the most severe form of penalty, whether in the form of time-out consequences for preschoolers or solitary confinement for the incarcerated. Disconnection does not only arise from physical separation, though; in many cubicle hallways, close proximity does not necessarily translate into mutual trust. Even when surrounded by others, individuals can feel intensely lonely and lack the support of those around them. Even in a vacuum, the brain is still emotional.

Emotionless workplaces often begin with the best of intentions. It all seems quite straightforward: generous benefits offered here and there, bonuses to keep people happy, a nice list of rules against hurting other people or stealing from the company, and easy parking. Sounds like it should be enough.

It isn't.

As long as a company intends to use humans within the business model, there will be a need for emotional connectedness in the business model. In the absence of an emotional strategy, a company exists in an emotional vacuum. Frontline workers and executives may experience individual joys and disappointments, but there isn't a *company experience* that unites the group. Colleagues function in parallel isolation rather than a cohesive emotional environment.

For a while, a company may succeed without formal attention to emotional strategy. Market share, popularity buzz, growth, and other measures of success may simply reflect the intrinsic value of the goods or services provided. People feel happy about results and enjoy the tides that have brought them fortunes. It seems like the good times will never end.

The upward trajectory continues until an unforeseen event shocks the system: a safety-related death, a shutdown by regulators, a slowdown compared to shareholder expectations, superstars leaving for better offers, key suppliers going bankrupt, or a streak of successful launches ends with a dud. Addressing such shocks requires risk mitigation strategies developed in advance, and most companies review such possibilities within their planning processes.

For a company with an emotional connectedness vacuum, what typically follows such an event is a mix of shame, blame, hostility, finger pointing, terminations, revoked promises, withdrawn funds, jockeying for position among leaders, micromanagement, decision hesitation, doubt, and suspicion. These represent the fight-flight-freeze reactions ("F" responses). Typically, companies have *not* factored such possibilities into their planning processes.

Without an emotional strategy that frames how a group coalesces, the company leaves itself open to emotional implosion. Things will get worse and such events will continue if the company does not address emotional issues.

If emotional strategy is a beautiful house on a nice street left vacant, disaster feels personally invited to squat.

The "F" Responses

The fable of Hypothetical Studios illustrates the third step in the downward sequence (fight-flight-freeze) between being an emotionless company and facing business doom from emotional destruction.

Hypothetical Studios was finally hitting its stride, with four of its last five releases earning critical acclaim along with healthy earnings. So with great expectations, both critics and financiers were eager to hear the opening-weekend results of the latest offering from the hottest little place in Hollywood.

And to their dismay, the film finished ninth at the box office.

Even with a well-known star and a generous marketing budget, the quiet family drama could not outperform its competitors. Two action blockbusters from other studios were also premiering the same weekend, and shocking tabloid reports of a celebrity extramarital affair (completely unrelated to any of the films) stole away the buzz that Hypothetical was hoping to generate for its latest project. Timing was not kind to the team.

Angela, Andrew, and Albert were in their offices when the disappointing final numbers came early on Monday morning. As the chiefs of development, production, and marketing, they would be held responsible for the disaster. Dozens of junior and senior colleagues would instantly be worried about the fate of the studio and whether other projects would still be green-lighted to proceed.

Angela storms into Andrew's room where Albert is also sitting. In an angry tone, she begins to chastise her peers.

"I can't believe you are so disorganized! How could you two be so stupid? Didn't you look at the calendar? How did you ever get this job anyway? And I'll tell you one more thing, they are *not* going to pin this disaster on me!"

Somewhat dumbfounded at the attack, Andrew starts to tune out Angela's words after the first minute. He instinctively wants to run away to clear his head. He gets up to leave the room when the other two tell him to sit down. Andrew begins to ponder his next move in a different company.

As the most experienced of the three, Albert is a mentor to many. He joined Hypothetical as a fresh start after many years at one of the large studios. Colleagues around the office frequently ask for his advice, and he is known for his terrific instincts in making snap judgments. He has a remarkable feel for the business. Today, his confidence is deeply shaken. While he's had bombs before, he's never encountered such a gap between expectations and results. He now doubts his ability to decide what to have for lunch, let alone how to make a motion picture successful. He isn't sure he can make the right choices anymore.

It is only one really bad day for a bad project, but the cascade of emotional effects on three senior team members sets into motion a further decline of Hypothetical Studios.

Angela begins to abrasively battle everyone, frequently scolding assistants and coworkers ("Shut up and do what I say!" and "Am I the only one who cares about doing a good job anymore?"). She refuses to give up one dime of her budget or hour of her talent resources to work on other parts of the business, despite pressing needs elsewhere. Andrew begins missing meetings, and neither his assistant nor anyone else can reach him. He states that he is dealing with personal problems, but production slows and decisions are delayed nonetheless in his absence. Albert experiences the greatest shift of the three, as his former alacrity with decisions has now slowed to a sleepy crawl. He ponders every risk of every decision to a detailed level, frightened to make another bad choice. Even in meetings where he is the decision maker, he repeatedly calls for additional meetings to discuss possible options.

The fable of Hypothetical Studios began as a story of promise: top talent, plentiful capital, good ideas, and experienced managers. Yet, without an emotional strategy promoting connectedness, a single difficult event triggered all three sets of fight-flight-freeze responses. Tempers flare while others retreat, and empty meetings occur where no progress is made.

As the environment gets worse, a paradoxical effect occurs: organizations tend to respond with *more* of the difficult practices (i.e., the three Fs) that have made things bad in the first place. When things are going down, they try more of the same. The sales group that falls short of forecast because of a hostile manager will likely engender even more hostility from that manager. The unit that misses a deadline because of oppressive micromanagement will receive even more micromanagement. (This reflex is illogical. If an urgent task force cannot achieve all its objectives because of significant time spent preparing twice-a-week steering committee update documents, is the solution really daily updates?) The operations team not receiving decision input from fleeing or frozen superiors will face operating bottlenecks, making even bigger decisions necessary, which will likely trigger even more fleeing and freezing. All three F responses tend to intensify over time in such crescendo loops.

In many businesses without an emotional strategy, *the intended cure is more of the disease itself.* They address a problematic situation with more of the things that caused the problem, fighting a fire by pouring gasoline on it. What is needed instead is a new emotional foundation (more on that at the end of this chapter).

For companies where the freeze response has become widespread, decision sluggishness has the potential to accelerate the demise of the business. When decisions are not made promptly, crucial sales and operational actions cannot proceed.

One particularly ineffectual approach triggered by shock events is the all-in-one decision group, which coalesces smaller meetings into one large meeting so as to not miss crosscutting details. Ordinary boundaries are dissolved to accommodate transparency following an unexpected event. Unfortunately, this common approach has the tendency to backfire, as various topics receive inadequate attention from being bucketed with unrelated matters. For example, in a company where four functional groups blend with five product groups into one large turnaround team, the twenty interfaces each receive less time and focus than they did previously, and together they cannot effectively make decisions. (For a matrix organizational chart where functions are drawn in blue and products or geographies are drawn in red, creating one team to make every decision together can be referred to as a "dilution of the purple.") In contrast, the best way to navigate through a difficult period is to gradually build trust through efficient decision making in smaller groups supplemented by selected large group gatherings (see Chapter Eight).

Greed and Punishment: Paths to Destruction

The fourth step of the descent to emotional destruction is the adoption of either of the two anticonnectedness strategies: greed or punishment. The fifth and final step of the sequence is the eventual self-destruction that occurs from resource depletion resulting from these strategies.

After a company without an emotional strategy begins to encounter chaos (like Hypothetical Studios), it may choose to embrace a pessimistic view of workers. Leaders will begin to characterize employees in the most negative of terms. Behavior is reduced to simple rewards and punishments, and clichés such as carrots-and-sticks, incentives-and-disincentives, and shocks-and-silver are offered as tactics to improve performance. People are presumed to work harder only out of avarice or fear. The implicit assumption is that individual workers do not desire trust or connectedness to their colleagues; instead, they are selfish and self-motivated individuals who only produce when they are faced with extreme rewards or extreme threat—in other words, greed or punishment.

Of course, people *do* respond to greed. Money is a strongly seductive element that has corrupted many individuals and groups. The chance to become extremely wealthy has led many to forgo ethics, a sense of duty, and connectedness to others. In an environment where people have been dehumanized and don't trust anyone around them, greed will temporarily lead to improved results. The reflexive response of a company that has employed a greed strategy will be to throw bonuses at every problem. However, salary functions like a drug in the absence of emotional connectedness. The addict requires more and more to get her fix; a standard bonus brings diminishing emotional returns. You need to compensate more and more, just to stay where you are. At a certain point, there isn't enough to stay motivated.

138

Greed, just as any other addiction, warps individual judgment and risk tolerance. This eventually leads to the destruction of a business (i.e., step five of the sequence) when resources are embezzled, diverted to projects supporting individual gain over company gain, diverted to high-reward projects with excessive risk, and UPT creates internal sabotage.

Of course, people also respond to punishment. A worker fears the loss of his or her job, particularly if he or she has financial commitments, such as family. If sufficiently afraid, the employee is willing to endure (and even support) actions that violate his or her sense of dignity, ethics, morality, identity, and integrity. Bullying and humiliation are frequently part of the punishment management style; such behaviors from anyone are bad but coming from a boss are especially brutal. The reflexive response of a company that has employed a punishment strategy is to keep people feeling insecure about everything. Managers desire to create insecure overachievers in order to maximize productivity. Workers will remain with such an organization as long as they perceive the pain of unemployment is worse than the pain of staying.

When managers continually repress autonomy or skill expansion to prove to workers "who's the boss," then eventually the workers' desire and pursuit of excellence diminishes. (Some managers may note the contrary example of the worker who needed to be challenged or insulted in order to become motivated; this tends to work only in the short term until such insults create frustration rather than impetus.) It is exhausting for workers to put forth ideas and effort if the only result is rejection. They will do just enough to keep their job but never feel fortunate.

Punishment also leads to the self-destruction of a business. Excessive fear leads to decision hesitancy, micromanagement, and mistake avoidance rather than action. Innovation cannot occur because no one feels secure enough to test a new idea. Make people scared to try, and they stop trying. Eventually, there is no demand for yesterday's product and the company shrinks into oblivion.

The answer is not simply to avoid greed and punishment (or mix them in small doses rather than extremes). *Fear and avarice inevitably grow in companies when no good emotional alternative is available to the organization.* The answer is to build trust and emotional connectedness through one of the nine strategies.

Emotional Resuscitation of a Company

Overwhelming fight-flight-freeze or greed/punishment tactics are precursors to the demise of an organization. Once they have become the core culture of an organization, they are difficult to remove. One cannot simply turn on a new emotional strategy tomorrow, even if coming as a directive from the board or CEO; attempts at suddenly introducing emotional connectedness will fail from the pervasive absence of trust. As such, companies must require an *emotional resuscitation program* to set it on a new course.

The process of emotional resuscitation is analogous to supporting a patient following a prolonged serious surgery. To fully help the patient, first extract the cause of the disease (e.g., parasite, tumor, blood clot), allow the body to rest immediately, give adequate time for recuperation with support, and then rehabilitate the body to be active again with new skills.

Similarly, helping a company to ameliorate an entrenched destructive environment first requires an extraction of the problem. This typically means immediately ending practices that promote greed/punishment and the F responses. Prior compensation incentives are suspended, as are protocols that make enemies of business units. Leadership must convene in many cases to announce such a shift. In some cases, particularly toxic managers must be dismissed. A bold declaration and acknowledgment of the previously destructive path stops the descent to failure. To rebuild confidence after a disaster, acknowledge what went wrong in precise terms, articulate how it eroded trust, and convey the need for connectedness.

Next, the company needs time to recover. This may require shutting down the business for a short time (e.g., days or weeks) to bring groups of employees and executives together to discuss the emotional destruction occurring in the company. This can be a multiday town hall meeting followed by small group conversations to discuss the company; it is often a cathartic process. Engaging emotional counselors or facilitators can be helpful to some organizations where people have been historically reticent to share their frustrations. As I will review in Chapter Nine, listening is necessary for healing.

The process of recuperation then involves defining a new emotional strategy of connectedness (from the nine choices). The organization needs to specify how such practices will translate into operations and talent management (as described in Chapter Six). A task force can lead the process but should include company-wide engagement so that everyone can contribute to the vision of the company.

Lastly, after implementing practices, it is necessary to have follow-up discussions (as rehabilitation) to ensure that the chosen strategy is working. Such discussions can also provide feedback for course corrections.

* * *

How Now

- *Be better at decisions.* If decision making has been particularly difficult for an organization, then training leaders in the *five needs for decision making* can be particularly useful. They are:

  1. Trigger: "Let's end discussion and vote."
  2. Menu: "Have we identified all the options?"
  3. Facts: "Let's run the numbers and get the data."

4. Implications: "What are the risks? Do we have a plan B?"
5. Mechanism: "Is this a vote or consensus?"

If a meeting feels stuck without progress, someone needs to be the trigger person. If only one option is being debated, then someone needs to present a broader menu. If logic is being used in a discussion but data are being ignored, someone has to bring forth the facts. If a meeting is avoiding discussion of the downside risks, someone has to raise the red flag to consider the worst-case scenario. If there is silence after a decision has been called for, then someone should suggest the mechanism.

- *Change things from the ground up.* If you are in an organization that is on an emotionally destructive path, seek training for your group or unit to reduce the F responses. Create networks across the company, apply the nine emotional strategies locally within teams, form a catalyst group to improve company culture, and provide emotional feedback to those you supervise.

- *Use data.* Define costs associated with the emotionally destructive environment (e.g., staff replacement costs) in order to convince others that the company needs change for the financial health of the business.

- *Reduce unfair surprises and broken promises.* With each person with whom you work, reduce the incidence of unfair surprises and broken promises. Eliminating these two destroyers of trust from the workplace helps greatly to restore confidence in each other.

Chapter Eight:
Change the Oil in
Seven Languages

This chapter describes the role of leaders in shaping an integrated emotional archetype across the enterprise, using four forms of gatherings and blended expression formats.

Bookstores have thousands of inspirational, biographical, self-help, analytical, and psychological characterizations of leadership and how to lead others toward an outcome.

With that backdrop, *Emotional Business* will add another branch to the bonfire. Leadership is the *set of practices* that promote a *shift of group neurochemistry*. Leaders are the symphonic conductors of trillions of neurons, ensuring the flow of the right amounts of dopamine, serotonin, and numerous unseen substances.

Thankfully, such leadership does not require ingesting psychedelic drugs or opening skulls to perform experimental surgery! By *gathering* and *engaging*, leaders unite people through triggering of different emotional centers of the brain.

Importantly, this definition of leadership means that anyone can lead others toward great achievement if that person understands the methods by which groups are truly brought together and emotions influenced.

Changing the Oil

Gatherings create congregational clarity and endeavor endurance. The biggest achievements in history are the result of group effort. From the survival of hunter-gatherer villages to the worldwide social movements of today, the human condition is shaped by aggregated intent. Whether for financial, humanitarian, spiritual, or other objectives, leaders serve as intense magnets for stakeholders to assemble and forge bonds.

Within a company, though, daily pressures of the business model seem to preclude bringing people together. Departments in a large organization often complain to senior management about full calendars and that they would prefer to just do their own thing and not be bothered by wasting time in meetings (off-site or otherwise), training, town halls, or other convening events. Some will also offer that key performance indicators don't make forgiving allowances for time spent at gatherings.

Asking "why gather?" is, in many ways, the same as asking why an automobile owner should have the engine oil changed every x months or y-thousand miles. A relatively new car is running fine, so why should the owner spend precious time and money on it? Some will counter, "Because the owner's manual says so." True, but *right now the car is running fine*. So why do it? Another set of voices will offer, "Because it is good for long-term health of the car." True, but *right now the car is running fine*. So why do it? Finally, the revealing answer is, "Because even though it is running fine now, if you don't change the oil it will *lose its value* and problems build up." So, auto owners change the oil.

The same reasoning holds true for gathering members of an organization together. Without periodic stops in the calendar to refresh the substances that lubricate internal interfaces and minimize frictional destruction, the organization will fail in its aspirations and lose its value. Leaders gather people together to appraise the essentials of their connectedness, and in doing so they change the emotional oil for the organization.

Gathering people together is most important to do *when the organization is running fine,* to make sure it stays that way.

Across all cultures, gatherings take on four formats:

1. Thinking events, which emphasize problem solving or philosophical pondering
2. Enjoyment events, which engage people through enthusiasm or laughter
3. Act-for-change events, which utilize services for a greater cause as a means of creating shared identity
4. Reflection events, which center on gratitude and preservation of legacy

Some of these four are reminiscent of broader emotional strategies (discussed in Chapter Six); the distinction here is that all four event formats can and should occur within any of the nine emotional strategies.

In *thinking events,* a group comes together to talk, listen, exchange ideas, and utilize cognitive skills. The emotional impact of solving a problem together is reinforcing of group bonds, especially if the problem requires input from people of different backgrounds and perspectives to solve. Either the group leader or an external facilitator organizes the questions/topic/challenge for the group to solve. The participants can exchange ideas within large group sessions and small group sessions, as part of the thinking time.

Enjoyment events bring a group together to share in a happy or uplifting experience. Group meals, movies, karaoke, ball games, playful competitions, and amusement park trips all qualify. Laughter is a key component. Group enjoyment also enhances memory of the event, as people will reminisce with great fondness years later, "Do you remember that time when we all …?" Moments when people smile together strengthen singular group identity.

Act-for-change events help colleagues within the company, citizens within the community, or a vulnerable population. These might be service volunteerism (e.g., feeding the homeless at a soup kitchen) or advocacy (e.g., putting up posters for a particular cause). Brain chemistry provides pleasure for the act of altruism (i.e., it feels good to do good). This response heightens in doing so with others, as the joy of giving creates group convergence.

Reflection events allow people to come together to appreciate recent experiences, legacy, opportunities, strengths, wisdom, and resources within the group. People are connected by what they've commonly experienced or collectively received. For example, various professional services firms invite alumni to annual reunions to see old friends (and occasionally form new business arrangements as well). Retirement parties link the old with the new and can have the effect of inspiring younger workers regarding their own potential (e.g., "I want to have a long career and loyal friends like Marvin"). Memorial services for those who have recently died also have the effect of forcing attendees to see the value of their connections.

Rites of passage in various cultures combine the thinking, enjoyment, act-for-change, and reflection formats. For example, the bar mitzvah, confirmation, and *upanayanam* ceremonies signify the ascent from childhood to maturity but combine elements from the four gathering types as well. Each ceremony includes a recitation of faith principles, a celebration including food and music, some form of service or sacrifice for others, and a moment of observance of remembrance for deceased ancestors. Weddings include scriptural readings, receptions that include dancing until late-night hours, and champagne toasts to express thanks to friends or family; in recent years, couples have asked guests to make charity donations in lieu of gifts.

Within a business, the four gathering elements can serve as a checklist for events. For example, a company off-site might include agenda items, such as:

Thinking:
- Trivia competition about the company's customers
- Prioritization of the biggest challenges facing the company

Enjoyment:
- Humorous limerick writing about company products
- Skit performed by IT department about software rollout

Act for change:
- Competition to assemble toy packages for poor children
- Spending two hours off-site on local park cleanup

Reflection:
- Discussions about "the biggest lesson I've learned about sales from someone else in the group"
- A tribute to a company founder who recently died

Speaking in Seven Languages

Assembling people together does not alone influence group neurochemistry; a leader needs to use multiple formats of expression to trigger emotional brain responses. Words shape the way people feel about information and experiences.

Humans utilize seven formats of verbal expression ("seven languages") to engage with others:

1. Numbers
2. Logical arguments
3. Future state vision/outcome
4. Promises
5. Myth/story/example
6. Humor/evoking smiles and laughter
7. Empathy

Leaders vary in their comfort with using each of these, but their *collective* use is what enables influence. The more brain areas they reach means more emotional effect. A presentation that utilizes only facts and logic will have an academic or analytical feel to it and will only reach a fraction of a heterogeneous audience. A speech filled primarily with promises and humor may motivate a group but will not trigger neuro-emotional chemistry changes that foster group connectedness. The blend of all seven is the key, whether for communications with business, political, spiritual, or sales audiences.

People perceive *numbers* differently from approximations; for example, "63 percent" inherently feels different from "most." Numbers can create subtle emotional perceptions of abundance, precision, and diligence. People often use numbers in defense of assertions in logical arguments.

Logic is the technique of building conclusions from already accepted truth. Logical arguments are complex constructions using the basic building block of "If A, then B." When a leader presents ideas in a structured manner, he or she improves the chances of gaining the trust of an initially skeptical audience.

Future state descriptions organize groups around a common priority by stimulating group imagination. "Once this plan is implemented, we will all have P and Q." Future possibilities unite an audience through ideals, such as prosperity, excellence, hope, advancement, fairness, justice, mercy, security, or growth, often using the invocation of time (e.g., someday, afterward, in x years, when we are through this period, etc.). Future states can be presented in inspirational verbiage as well as more matter-of-fact ways (e.g., "We believe we can reach zero medical errors in our hospital within three years").

Promises are descriptions of future states for individuals in the audience, rather than the organization as a whole. Promises make it clear why an individual should align with the group from the view of *self-interest* (i.e., safety and security). In the context of a business discussion, the promises might be in relation to job status, wealth creation, freedom from specific burdens, or improved working conditions. The words must speak to the "what's in it for me?" question on each person's mind.

Myths, stories, and examples are the most universal of the seven language formats. All cultures throughout history have found connectedness (i.e., group neurochemistry) through the use of example, allegory, legend, and anecdote. Humans have an innate desire for story; even young babies will sit in rapt attention of an adult who voices a nursery rhyme. The greatest of influencers have understood this power; Buddha and Jesus taught with parables. Business leaders often boost audience engagement by beginning public comments with a story of a particular employee or customer.

Humor can be challenging to use appropriately without offending sections of an audience. Obviously, there is no place in modern business for jokes about gender, ethnic background, disability, sexual orientation, age, weight, or other personal attributes. Such utterances can be profoundly destructive to emotional connectedness. Humor is also fraught with risks; for every group there are specific topics one should avoid (e.g., layoffs from prior restructuring, compensation freezes, disease pandemics, national tragedies). Accepting those warnings, the application of humorous anecdotes, wit, wordplay, cute imagery, or other techniques to evoke smiles and laughter are very useful in creating group connectedness. Many business leaders begin public comments with a joke to lower defensiveness within the crowd.

Empathy is the act of expressing emotional states for creating group engagement. Speaking openly about emotional vulnerabilities has the potential to create engagement. You can articulate empathy in an array of relationship frames, from direct sympathy ("I feel your pain") to vulnerable disclosure ("Ten years ago, my sadness over my divorce made it hard to come to work") to determination ("I know this economic uncertainty is scary for all of us, but we will get through it").

As I noted earlier, it is the *blend* of these seven expression formats that enable communication to influence connectedness and group neurochemistry.

Additional possibilities for each category include:

Numbers
- Percentages
- Proportions
- Dollars
- Rarity ("only 3 in a million")
- Targets ("5 this year, 10 next year, 20 the year after that")

Logic
- "If, then" structure
- Catchy sayings of common sense
- Take an agreed-upon premise to its inevitable conclusion

Vision
- What will things look like?
- How will things work in the future?
- Whose suffering will be eased?

Promises
- Greater benefits
- Greater rewards
- Fewer problems
- Easy transition

Stories
- A character who overcomes a struggle
- Lesson learned the hard way
- Ideal way to handle a problem
- Situation all of us have been in
- Easily repeatable reference case

Humor-Smiles
- Funny picture or photo
- Cute picture of babies or animals
- Silly story that is not offensive
- Poem or song that includes references to group members

Empathy
- Allow your feelings to show
- Describe your awareness of the suffering of others

Consider the following example of blending the seven expression formats

Example: Restarting the Factory after Shutdown

Nancy is the plant manager for a cookie company. Inspectors recently ordered temporary closure of the production facility until multiple quality issues are corrected. She gathers the four hundred workers of the facility in a town hall meeting to galvanize the group.

"As all of you know, this has been a difficult time for our site. The excellence we've taken for granted for many years has been called into question, and that means we have to change the way we view our roles and operate.

"We have standard operating procedures for 9,278 activities within our production lines. The inspectors have pointed out changes for 181 of them. One hundred eighty-one changes might sound like a lot, but it's only correcting 2 percent of what we do. [Numbers]

"I don't look at this situation as a failure of effort or a failure of our people to do the right thing. It's a failure to adapt our systems. We began decades ago as a much smaller company with only a few products. Now we make dozens of items with much more complex systems. We updated machines and ingredients over the years, but we didn't update how we managed internal controls. That caught up to us; we simply outgrew the capacity of our small quality assurance team to keep up with everything. That's actually easy to fix. If the problem is an overburdened team, then we grow the team and streamline their workload. [Logic]

"I believe that our best days are not behind us but ahead of us. We are seeing tremendous appetite for our products in Asia and South America, and I see a day in the near future where we double our outputs on new production lines to meet the world's desire for our outstanding offerings. [Future state vision]

"With all the bad news in the local papers and the rumor mill, it would be natural to ask whether you'll still have a job here. What I can say to you is that you definitely have a job today, but whether we can maintain our size is completely dependent on how fast we get back to producing and bringing in revenue. If we all take on the challenge to correct the inspector's concerns, then I'm sure there will be a place for all of us. [Promise]

"I want to share with you one example of how we all need to approach this situation. Our packaging engineer, Nate Thompson, got a call late on Friday afternoon from an equipment supplier in Toledo that one of the vital components didn't get included with the shipment load that went out on Friday morning. It turns out the rest of the shipment was useless without that one component. So rather than having his improvement installation delayed, Nate drove all night to Toledo in his van and hauled the components all the way back here himself. That kind of dedication brings a smile to my face. [Story]

"It also makes me smile to think about all the silly ways that customers have been telling the company that they want our products back on the shelves. One guy in Belgium sent in a creative amateur video of aliens taking cookies to their home world, with the tagline, 'Aliens have stolen our cookies, so we need to make more here on Earth!' The crazy things people do … [Humor]

"To close on a serious note, I know that this is not an easy time for any of us here. We feel tired and overwhelmed by all that is asked of us, and it isn't going to get easier anytime soon. It doesn't feel fair that we should have to invest so much. When you are here on evenings and weekends trying to make things right, please know that I understand your sacrifice. [Empathy]

"In the end, I know that the challenges facing us are small hurdles compared to the grand abilities of our outstanding people. Thank you for everything that you do, seen and unseen, to keep our momentum going. Soon, we will look back on this as a small bump in a fantastic road ahead."

* * *

How Now

- *Schedule a gathering to change the oil.* Bring the managers of the organization together to discuss emotional strategy and forming connectedness within the organization. Use all four types of gatherings (thinking, enjoyment, act-for-change, and reflection) to create the highest impact on emotional cohesiveness.

- *Adapt internal communications to include all seven language formats.* Internal initiatives often emphasize numbers and logic in updates, but employees across the organization require promises, future vision, examples, humor, and empathy as well to fully embrace messages.

- *Adapt external communications to include all seven language formats.* Shareholders, regulators, governments, customers, community residents, activists, and suppliers each have an agenda that they wish to impose on a company. Adjusting communications to include all seven formats allows for greater influence with each group.

- *Manage upward using seven formats.* Leaders not only speak to those lower in the hierarchy but to their bosses as well. To minimize micromanagement and maintain healthy communication upward, share information and updates using all seven formats. Give your boss some numbers, a case example, a humorous anecdote, a vision of how things are coming together, and other formats to create trust.

Chapter Nine:
The Ear Is Mightier than
the Sword

This chapter discusses the central role of listening in business practices.

Why do humans speak with each other? We do it from our earliest days. Even babies babble to other babies, as evidenced by the countless viral videos of infant siblings muttering to each other before they have vocabulary or syntax.

It is the human survival mechanism through all experiences to *feel together*, and listening is a shared response to events uplifting and tragic. Just as neurochemistry shifts for an organization from gathering and blending expression formats, listening generates the same effect between two individuals.

The survival mechanism of connectedness extends beyond simple sharing of food or shelter; we feel compelled to relate about things that make us angry, scared, uncertain, confused, joyful, or overwhelmed. Intense experiences make us want to share and connect (e.g., the married corporate executive who beams with pride while telling her husband of her promotion, the enraged customer who calls to complain about a defect in his recent expensive purchase). Verbalizing our inner states to others connects us to them.

Hearing versus Listening

The terms "hearing" and "listening" are used interchangeably, when in fact they represent two entirely different processes.

Hearing is a passive sensory step-by-step process. Even when you don't want to, hearing occurs. Sound is generated by the disruption of air particles by forces in the environment; the ear detects the subsequent waves of particle movement. The eardrum and inner ear machinery convert this energy flow into electrical signals, which transmit through the eighth cranial nerve to the brain stem and the auditory cortex of the superior temporal lobe. Abracadabra, we hear!

Listening is an active emotional step-by-step choice. Listening occurs only when you intentionally desire to listen. The potential listener's ears and eyes detect signals. Then, a potential listener chooses whether to devote further attention to someone's need. The speaker expresses verbal and nonverbal communication and triggers numerous brain areas to understand. Abracadabra, we listen!

The distinction between these two phenomena is often a source of friction between parties. One party will accuse, "You're not listening!" when the other party is merely hearing. Even the most innocuous of a listener's nonverbal microbehaviors, such as glancing away to look at a watch during a conversation, can convey a lack of interest and cause the speaker to become irritated. Customers are offended if they perceive a company employee is obligatorily hearing rather than listening to (and addressing) the customer concern.

Listening is an inherited mechanism of emotional connection to those around us; babies know how to listen! While cynical socialization may inculcate inferior behaviors, such as manipulation, coercion, inducing guilt, or indifference, it is in the instincts of our species to be drawn to those who welcome rather than use weapons. The ear is mightier than the sword.

Six Tools in a Toolbox

One tool never suffices for all situations. You cannot only use IT upgrades to solve all supply chain issues. You cannot cure all infections with penicillin. To properly address a problem, you must have a toolbox from which to choose the right tool for the right circumstance.

Despite the need for flexible tools that match business circumstances, training programs have unfortunately portrayed listening as a one-technique-fits-all behavior. Nod the head, make eye contact, and ask the occasional clarifying question. Listening 101.

As the sophistication of emotional recognition increases in business, there must be more than one effective way to listen, as there is more than one reason that people need to be listened to. The irate daughter of a dying hospital patient should not receive the same listening response as a disappointed customer returning a defective product.

There are six circumstances where humans desire to be heard and, thus, six very different forms of listening required:

1. Release of anger
2. Fast fulfillment of a need
3. Affirmation in periods of uncertainty/fear
4. Problem solving support
5. Shared joy
6. Supportive nurturance during pain

Every human will be a "speaker" in each of these situations at some point. Who among us has not felt rage, urgency, uncertainty, confusion, exhilaration, and pain? All of us will be in these circumstances, which means that each of us can be a listener as well for these circumstances.

Each of these circumstances requires a listener to have a different mind-set, nonverbal practices, and verbal responses. The goal is to engage as a listener in the right rhythm.

This situation-dependent framework for listening also redefines what it means to be a great listener. Rather than simply excelling at one form of listening, the great listener understands when to *switch* techniques dependent on the speaker's emotional needs. Many times an intense conversation may require a listener to bounce among the six styles at unpredictable points.

For professionals whose job description includes a heavy component of interacting with emotional individuals (e.g., employee supervisors, retail clerks, police officers, nurses, therapists, social workers, human resources personnel, customer service representatives), traditional training in only one form of listening may be inadequate to address the complex emotional pressures faced by those they serve. It is better to have more options than penicillin.

Listening #1: Release of Anger

It is important to distinguish the internal experience of *anger*, a reflexive experience sometimes impossible to control, versus the *release of anger*, a behavior that you must control in business contexts, as it can hurt others. Anger is an umbrella term that encompasses internal sensations of annoyance, irritation, frustration, rage, and antagonism. Release of anger can include behaviors such as screaming alone, using profanity, bellowing frustrations, scolding someone, punching a hard object, disrupting order (e.g., shoving papers off a desk), and other physical releases of pent-up intensity. "Anger management" is probably a misnomer, as it implies the ability to control internal feelings. "Managing release of anger" might be more precise.

You can't always control what you feel, but you can control what you do with those feelings.

We gradually learn anger-releasing behaviors through parenting, socialization, and experience within a particular educational or work environment. While some workplace environments have tolerated shouting as an acceptable release of anger, such behavior is increasingly unacceptable due to the contagious toxic effects on others in the workplace.

So, if an individual is angry, most of the outward means of releasing the anger are not permitted. Instead, individuals are primarily afforded the chance to talk about their frustrations.

*Listener mind-set to speaker anger: As a listener to an enraged individual, think of the mnemonic HVAC: heating, ventilation, air conditioning. If they are *heated*, let them *vent* their frustrations until they *cool down*. The goal is not to stop them from shouting but to let them fully exhaust all the hot air. It will take all of your abilities as a calming force to bring them calmness as well. This requires patience.

*Listener nonverbal response to speaker anger: The best way to listen to angry individuals is to stay perfectly still while letting them shout until the fire burns itself out. Listener stillness brings calmness to the situation. If angry individuals encounter even small listener movements, such as gestures, head nodding, or touch, then they continue to shout. They are primed for a fight and movement/contact stimulates the fight to continue. Simply let them finish. They will often apologize once they run out of steam and feel regretful that they became so hostile. Orient your body toward them, stay still and calm, and keep your face neutral (more so than smiling or looking intense).

*Listener verbal response to speaker anger: Don't ever interrupt angry individuals when they are in the middle of the tirade by telling them to calm down; it is only going to escalate the drama of the situation. If you do, they are likely to counter with, "Don't tell me to calm down! I'm not the one with the problem—you are!" An angry individual typically finishes venting within thirty seconds if the listener is still. After the angry speaker stops to catch his breath, pause for a considerable time to let the air clear. Then, offer an empathetic reply, as he is vulnerable in the post-shouting period. If he is upset over something of pain and worry (e.g., a sick family member), then a response acknowledging that pain is appropriate (e.g., "I can tell this situation is really upsetting you"). If he is angry due to disappointment in an expensive product or service, then a solution-oriented statement is appropriate (e.g., "Let's discuss what would correct this").

Listening #2: Urgent Fulfillment of a Need

We feel the pressure of urgency for a variety of reasons: others are waiting for us to deliver something (e.g., reports, sales figures), we sense a diminishing window of opportunity (e.g., the deal is gone tomorrow), or we want to end a deprivation/discomfort (e.g., needing heat restored in an building with a broken furnace).

Individuals experiencing such pressure tend to exude a mix of frustration, impatience, and worry. They are in a train about to hit a wall, and they need prompt action. They are likely to be abrupt in verbal exchanges as a result.

*Listener mind-set to speaker urgency: Individuals feeling pressure have two tracks simultaneously playing. On the first track, they are declaring their product/service/action *need* (e.g., "The charts on this sales forecast are wrong, and your team needs to fix them by noon"). On the other track, their nonverbal gestures make their emotional *anxiety* apparent (e.g., their body language is indicating, "Please do not let me be embarrassed in front of the CEO"). As a listener, one needs to absorb both tracks. Hear the words and respond to their verbal content, but also respond to the unexpressed worries evident in their voice inflections and agitated movements. Be careful not to interpret their anxiety as some form of attack on you; the tension in their voice is likely not directed at you but at the circumstances making them feel pressured.

*Listener nonverbal response to speaker urgency: These speakers do not feel secure, so make them feel secure with you. Make them nonverbally aware of your superhero strength: stand tall (stretch your neck toward the ceiling), stay fixed in your stance without fidgeting, and use determined facial expressions to convey readiness to face a challenge.

*Listener verbal response to speaker urgency: The speaker needs to be emotionally relieved of the anxiety (track two) *before* he is ready to hear the content/service detail (track one). Whether for the customer, colleague, acquaintance, or boss who approaches you with an urgent need, the first words to the person under pressure should be, "We'll make this right." A customer needs to hear, "I'll walk with you to our returns department to address this." The first thing a coworker or boss wants to hear is "This is a straightforward fix" or "Whatever it takes, let's get it done." Defer making apologies or explanations or offering the details of a product/ service until the *second* part of the interaction. Some urgently pressured customers will interrupt a response that begins with an apology, so verbalize *resolution before regret.*

Listening #3: Affirmation in Periods of Uncertainty/Fear

While some worries are urgent escalations (Listening #2), other worries are chronic concerns. In the prior listening approach, the technique was for the speaker to assure individuals that he would address their problem promptly. If the problem is not immediately resolvable, the listening technique must provide an alternate message.

A speaker with chronic worries needs space to unload his collective concerns to another person, and then (after the "dumping" has been accomplished) a mix of hope, affirmation, refocusing, compliments, and encouragement to go forward.

As I noted in Chapter Five, the human physiological response to threat is designed for short-term bursts rather than ongoing burdens. The longer an issue persists, the greater the need to verbally release accumulated anxieties. Situations that qualify for this form of listening are common: financial risks hanging over a person, unreasonable expectations, joblessness or job uncertainty, strained working relations, strained personal relationships, health problems, and so on. The things that keep you up at night are the province of listening style #3.

Such topics are not typically discussed openly because of their inherent magnitude and insolvability. The stigma associated with some topics may also create an air of embarrassment that inhibits reaching out to others for affirmation and support. They may wrongly believe they are the first and only executive/colleague/friend who has ever worried about a particular subject.

Since the listener is not in a position to solve the big problems, the listener's goal is to give the speaker a welcoming invitation to release whatever pent-up worries he is carrying.

*Listener mind-set to speaker worry: When a speaker approaches you with the appearance of anxiety, he may be embarrassed to initiate the conversation about what is concerning him because such topics are typically viewed as risky to reputation or status. The speaker may indirectly start a bland conversation about innocuous topics or already resolved work issues but secretly hope the *listener* will invite a deeper conversation ("Do you want to talk about something bothering you?"). The listener has to initiate the context in which the speaker can be unrestrained in expressing his suppressed anxieties. Be open and be nonjudgmental.

*Listener nonverbal response to speaker worry: The speaker enveloped in uncertainty may worry about being judged or dismissed as paranoid. As such, listening to a person dealing with fear/uncertainty requires a focused laser of undivided attention. Do not look away at a watch. Keep eyes directed on the speaker's eyes, and orient the body directly at the speaker. As part of the foundation for emotional disclosure, such microbehaviors convey the message of "Hey, don't worry about everybody else around. It's just you and me here." Gentle head nodding can also convey an acceptance of what the speaker is offering to the listener.

*Listener verbal response to speaker worry: Fairly little needs to be said as the speaker initially voices his concerns. Let him get it out. As the speaker concludes, he will typically ask for feedback; "Am I crazy?" and "I sound so stupid" are not uncommon. The speaker desires reassurance to persist in the face of ongoing uncertainty. Simple statements like "It makes sense that you'd be experiencing this, but remember you've got friends like me to help" can be unexpectedly elevating.

Listening #4: Problem Solving Support

Some problems are sufficiently intricate and necessitate engaging another person to help. This is particularly true when judgment or instinct, rather than data analysis, drives the decisions. Most decisions in ethics, career advancement, social relationships, parenting, and anything in unexplored territory require consideration of multiple consequences.

When problems are overwhelming, the emotional state of the speaker is typically confusion. There are so many pros and cons that the speaker is left "frozen," not knowing what to do next. For most people, these are situations where they seek to talk it out with a receptive listener.

*Listener mind-set to speaker confusion: If a person wants your advice and wisdom, she will ask for that directly. If instead she begins with, "I'm working through something tough, mind if I bounce a few ideas off you?" then she is not asking for your advice. She is asking for your *process help* in working with her so she can find *her own* answer. The listener in this circumstance must focus on asking rather than telling, being neutral rather than guiding. The speaker wants to talk it through.

*Listener nonverbal response to speaker confusion: This is a dance that the speaker leads. Follow her pace, move with her, and be her mirror image. She is most helped by feeling that a partner is moving with her. If she is energetically moving, then do so with her. If she is pensive and appears subdued, match her in that demeanor. Misalignment in this nonverbal element will often make the speaker feel isolated rather than that she is receiving help.

*Listener verbal response to confusion: The best response to the speaker in this situation is a series of questions. After the speaker explains the decision with which she's struggling, ask, "What do you think your options are?" Her subsequent response should be followed by another probing question or a summation question ("So you have four choices?"). The unrelenting focus on the speaker as the problem solver is usually appreciated. It may be tempting to provide guidance or a solution to the confused speaker. Yet, in this form of listening, it is more important for the speaker to find her own answer. If you're unclear about what she wants, then bluntly ask, "Do you want me to help you work through the question to find your answer, or do you want me to just tell you what I think?" In general, speakers will ask for the former more than the latter.

Listening #5: Shared Joy

Humans don't like to be happy alone. Teenagers immediately text their friends when something good happens. Couples espouse the expectation of sharing successful moments and would feel betrayed if not invited to be a part of the other's delight. Business victories are cherished within team celebrations. Humans feel joy together.

If joy is not shared in synchrony, then there is the potential for pain. Imagine a happy nine-month-old girl, able to sit and energetically crawl. She encounters simple things with a sense of wonder. One day she becomes particularly enthralled with a bright-purple ball. She then holds the ball and quickly scoots back to her nearby mother with excitement. If her beaming baby smile is met with cold neutrality because the mother is distracted, the smile immediately dissipates. She may try again several more times to express excitement and make her mother smile back at her. If the mother is not attuned to the child's emotional state, then the infant's joyous invitation is a futile undertaking. Eventually the infant will crawl away and perhaps lose interest in the ball that brought her so much joy only a few moments earlier. Both baby humans and adult humans find disappointment in unshared enthusiasm.

*Listener mind-set to speaker joy: It might sound obvious, but let the happy person have her moment. Be happy with her and for her. Regardless of how irrelevant or minor the source of happiness is, if a speaker comes to a listener with exuberance about something, she is hoping that the listener will engage in shared joy. She is not looking for analysis as to why the accomplishment may not be impressive. No one should be anything but authentic; if one cannot summon a smile to match the enthusiasm of the speaker, then politely excusing oneself is preferable to disappointing the speaker.

*Listener nonverbal response to speaker joy: This is a happy dance. Whatever they do, match them in the dance. If they have a big smile, then you offer a big smile. If they are waving their arms, then move your hands/arms/legs/feet to match their energy level (but not an identical copying of their movements). Physical contact, such as hugs or high fives are a common way of establishing connectedness in joy. In this listening style, nonverbal signals are a higher priority than spoken words.

*Listener verbal response to speaker joy: There are two forms of verbal communication necessary to convey shared joy. First, offer congratulations or expressions of significance (e.g., "That's terrific!" or "Wow, nicely done!"). Second, offer statements of emotional data (e.g., "You look so happy!" or "I'm so happy for you!").

Listening #6: Supportive Nurturance during Pain

There are moments when emotional devastation shocks those in our business circles: a colleague finds out he has pancreatic cancer, a coworker uncovers her spouse's infidelity, a longtime client sees his son being arrested on the television news for involvement in a financial swindle. Intense grief, betrayal, resentment, and a mix of many brain chemistry changes ensue. It creates vulnerability and emotional chaos within the individual.

In some unemotional workplaces, the expected response to learning of such troubling episodes is polite isolation (e.g., "I'm sorry if this is a tough time. Let me know if you need anything"). Showing support may be awkward.

Yet, for many people, the workplace is a hub of friendship. Emotional connectedness with colleagues supplements their loved ones as a source of goodness in their life. We spend the majority of our waking hours not with family, but with coworkers. Many people *want* to talk about the difficulties of their nonwork lives with those they trust at work, just as they might do the inverse.

Colleagues under such life pressures are not difficult to spot; first they may seem distracted in a meeting, and then they seem to fret during lunch, and finally they seem overwhelmed sitting at their desk. At last, they will knock on a colleague's door or ask to take a coffee break together to talk.

Potential listeners in such circumstances are sometimes intimidated by the challenge of supporting someone; the issues seem too big and outside their comfort zone. It is important to remember that individuals experiencing such grief are not asking for colleagues to be their rabbi or therapist; they simply want someone who will help them feel less alone.

*Listener mind-set to speaker pain: The goal of the listener here is to focus on the pain. If the speaker begins with a lengthy saga ("It all started eighteen years ago ..."), gently redirect the speaker to talk about his current emotional state. Talking too much about the past does not allow the speaker to move forward. Be reassuring that things will get better. Expect that the speaker may cry. Allow the speaker to fully release whatever anguish he has. Suppress physiological responses; avoid a statement like "Don't cry, you don't need to cry," as it inhibits the very release for which the speaker is yearning.

*Listener nonverbal response to speaker pain: This listening style is distinguished by the use of *touch* to support the listener. While all workplaces should follow all government restrictions about unwanted physical contact between work colleagues, it is reassuring when weeping to feel the sensation of *firm* *pressure against the forearm*. Of course, the listener must assess the emotional signals of the speaker before doing this. The listener may need to bluntly ask, "Do you want me to give you more space here?" to verify whether touch is welcomed before reaching over to make physical contact. Hugging is too intimate for a superficial acquaintance and should be reserved for a longtime contact, where deep trust exists. There is a curious phenomenon that people whisper when talking about emotional matters, even if they are all alone in a room; one can speculate that this is a biological instinct that forces the listener to move in closer to hear, which makes touch more accessible.

*Listener verbal response to speaker pain: Be expressive, sympathetic, and reassuring. There are only two phrases to avoid when listening to someone in a state of grief: (1) "I know how you feel," and (2) "Don't be so sensitive." With the first, the implication is that the listener has actually lived through the same experience as the speaker (if so, then use it). If someone who has not been through a similar situation uses the phrase, then the listener will typically retort, "You have no idea how I feel." With the second, the listener is usually intending to say, "I wish this didn't hurt you so much," but saying "don't be" implies that they are ordering the speaker to be less weak or vulnerable.

The Seventh Listening Style Is outside the Business Realm

The seventh circumstance (therapeutic listening) is where people call upon each other for healing from traumatic situations. PTSD is plentiful in human experience but fortunately rare in daily conduct of business. Thus, a further detailed discussion of therapeutic listening is not warranted (or adequately possible) in this text. It is the province of those with extensive training in social work, psychology, psychiatry, pastoral care, and counseling.

With that, business leaders and colleagues should be able to spot when someone in the company needs the specialized skills required to handle this particular form of listening support.

Individuals who have faced severe trauma will "not be themselves"; they may appear distracted, volatile, or have altered patterns of reactions to working conditions. One person may be newly withdrawn, while another may transform from a quiet monk to an aggressive antagonist. In essence, the neurochemistry of the individual has been disrupted, leading to a new set of emotional responses to business stimuli.

The obligation of managers and colleagues is to direct the affected individual to receive the specialized forms of listening (and other mental health services) required to reset the neurochemistry. In some organizations this is done through HR; in others it is part of employee assistance programs and may be provided by external partners.

The Clinton–Mandela Skills

Two of the best "leader listeners" are US President Bill Clinton and South African President Nelson Mandela. Whether shaking hands with audience members after a speech or greeting a foreign dignitary, these two leaders have the keen ability to form trust quickly.

If you observe them closely, Clinton and Mandela both exhibit five specific nonverbal listening microbehaviors that allow them to quickly generate emotional connection with individuals.

The five behaviors are eye contact, smiling, slowed cadence, inflections of voice volume, and touching the body center/torso of others.

Eye contact is simple to describe but difficult for many to consistently do during interactions. If the person is in your vicinity, then you should be looking at her eyes. Her clothing, jewelry, or body features may attract your initial attention from afar, but when in close proximity always keep your eyes on her eyes.

Smiling is the act of expressing joy and a pleasant mood through angling of the mouth; this can be with lips pursed or lips open to reveal teeth. When in close proximity, smiling provides a subtle cue that the other person feels comfortable with you. Defenses drop as a result. Strangers offer friendly smiles to each other on the streets of small villages, though this tends to shock the urban visitors.

Cadence is a musical term that denotes the emotional impact of velocity on performance. For a marching band, too fast feels anxious. Too slow feels melancholy. In one-on-one conversations, speaking too quickly will feel rushed and bureaucratic. For example, a call center representative who offers an initial speedy monotone greeting of "Thankyouforcalling you'reavaluedcustomer" does not apply the right cadence to convey the emotional intent. It feels obligatory rather than responsive, mechanical rather than emotional. When delivering particularly important information or in saying something particularly emotional, (pause) slow (pause) down.

Actors and politicians have been trained to vary their voice *volume* to achieve emotional impact. Loud, booming oratory will command attention and project attributes of strength, authority, and confidence. In contrast, whisperlike confessions and expositions of vulnerabilities mesmerize a group's attention and bring tears to the audience's eyes. Our brains are sensitized to the waves of louder and softer volumes that occur in storytelling.

Touch has the ability to quickly connect or quickly frighten a person. Touching the body center (face, chest) of a stranger at first meeting is typically considered invasive or rude, but the forearm and shoulder/upper back are usually nonthreatening and safe. To create greater connection, merge an initial handshake with the other hand, applying pressure to the forearm or shoulder blade. As long as it is culturally appropriate, the additional contact bolsters the intensity of the trust and connection.

What do these five microbehaviors have in common? They are utilized in forming emotional *attachments with babies.*

Consider how mothers and fathers all over the world engage with their infants in early periods of infancy. Adults make direct eye contact with infants, even holding them in their arms a few inches away, almost touching face-to-face.

Adults smile constantly at babies, in part hoping that they will smile back. Even when verbalizing unpleasant details, adults smile while saying, "You have such a smelly poopy diaper, my little angel baby!" The adult sounds happy despite the odor.

E v e r y w o r d i s s t r e t c h e d o u t in the cadence with babies. The infant pays greater attention to words said in a melodic, singsong manner than words spoken at the normal rate used adult to adult.

Adults vary their volume with babies. The words of a grumpy character in a story are voiced with dramatic crescendo, contrasting them with the gentle tones of normal play. Babies are fascinated by the *forte* and spellbound by the soft.

Adults all over the world use rubbing the shoulders and arms as a common means of massaging a crying infant. Touch is an emotionally soothing contact.

The fact that the youngest members of the species are so consistently charmed by these microbehaviors suggests that the five are part of our inborn neurological architecture of survival. When we communicate and listen as adults, connectedness is triggered by the use of eye contact, smiling, cadence, volume, and touch.

Interestingly, problems in these five microbehaviors also affect perception of personality. When we sense someone is "a bit different" or "not quite right," it is often because of small variations in his or her presentation of these five.

Breaking the Connection

What makes someone a "bad" listener?

The brain is the center of emotion and, thus, the center of listening capabilities. There are brain conditions that may inhibit interactive engagement (e.g., autism, Asperger's, Alzheimer's, brain tumors). Brain afflictions, such as addiction, also tend to reduce listening focus with others.

In other cases, broken connection is the result of using the wrong listening technique of the six situational approaches or insufficiently polished nonverbal microbehaviors (Clinton-Mandela skills).

For others, the ability to listen is constrained by other emotional burdens they currently face, which leave them exhausted (we don't always know what is going on in someone's personal life). Someone who appears to be a bad listener may simply be hiding the pain he or she is experiencing.

Lastly, for some people, good listening skills must replace a set of entrenched bad habits. They actually believe they're listening when, in fact, they're not. Interrupting, pressuring, competing, and intellectualizing all diminish trust in a listener.

* * *

How Now

- *Train executives in listening.* Leaders have two reasons to listen: (1) absorb key ideas from others and (2) shift group neurochemistry through connectedness. Even with the right desire, exceptional listening requires practiced skills to be effective. Hire a knowledgeable expert to teach the six listening styles to executives.

- *Train frontline associates in listening.* Create an expectation that every employee will know how to listen. This will help reduce frustrations within the company as well as improve interactions with customers.

- *Practice listening and Clinton-Mandela skills everywhere.* With the spouse, children, friends, the mailman, etc.

Chapter Ten:
We Live in Four Boxes

This chapter discusses the three sources of emotional stress in the workplace and the four categories of behavioral responses to stress.

It is 7:00 a.m. on a cold and dark February morning in the suburbs of Houston. At the headquarters of Hypothetical Incorporated, only a handful of employees have hurried in to begin their day at the early hour.

Among the early arrivers are senior managers Harriet, Hugo, Horace, and Helen. Each walks in the front door and acknowledges the security guard with a quick nod. With their briefcases in one hand and coffee in the other, they proceed down immaculately clean hallways, taking different turns past conference rooms and assorted cubicles. As they arrive a few moments later at their offices and hang their coats, their minds are already engaged in arithmetic and preparing for upcoming tough questions from the executive committee. Their expressiveness is muted, as the looming deadline is but three days away. Each must deliver his or her respective department's data for strategic planning. The CEO has personally spoken to each of them to emphasize the importance of their presentations, as the meeting will shape the organization for the next five years.

Cold winds blow outside, while emotional coolness circulates inside the building.

Helen joined the company thirty years ago as a mail clerk and now runs the largest division. Recruiters and managers repeat her story of career progression often to new employees for motivation. She remains steadfastly loyal to the company despite attractive offers to lure her away to become the CEO of smaller enterprises. She struggles emotionally with what she sees as an erosion of entrepreneurial values and mentoring over the past five years, particularly since the arrival of two new members on the board of directors. Her husband and three grown children have repeatedly heard, "This is not the company I joined," in multiple dinner conversations. An increasing emphasis on templates and bureaucratic documentation has diminished her unit's focus on innovation and opportunity hunting. She tries to follow the example set by her first mentor, Henry, who brought the division together in gatherings. A large checklist hangs in the central conference room, and different teams post daily updates to inspire the rest in a spirit of progress. Nonetheless, Helen feels an increasing need to call her husband several times each day just for him to make her laugh. She needs his humorous perspective as a syndicated cartoonist to get through this particularly unpleasant phase in her career.

Horace is concerned about budget cuts to his department. His efficiency over the past four years has now backfired on him, as senior management now wants to further reduce his funds, given how well he has maintained costs. He feels like he won a weight-loss contest and was rewarded with a wardrobe of lavish clothes two sizes too small. The entire product line that Horace manages is under competitive pressure from South America and Southeast Asia, further exacerbating the need to reshape his division. He wonders why he has to try so hard to win the basic company resources that other leaders come by so easily. His most recent year-end bonus resembled a meager cost-of-living increase rather than an incentive to continue his meticulous ways. His direct reports arrive shortly after Horace, ready for his onslaught of revisions and rewrites. They've dubbed him the "knight of nanomanagement" ("He's one thousand times worse than micromanagement"). Unbeknownst to colleagues, he is becoming addicted to online fantasy role-playing games as an escape from the perceived unpleasantness of his predicament.

Hugo is the youngest of the four senior managers. His tenacity combined with an against-the-grain intellectual talent has allowed the company to shift into new product arenas. His financial results are impressive. He feels pressure related to the upcoming meeting, nonetheless, as he senses that the inflection point is happening now to transition the company's philosophy from "legacy leaning" to "forward focused." While he is exceptionally blunt in telling people what he thinks, he is deeply private about his personal use of yoga, aromatherapy, and warm baths to physically renew.

Harriet is the vivacious natural leader to whom everyone is drawn. Educated at the premier institutions of Europe, she exudes confidence and radiates phenomenal intellectual capabilities. Her captivating smile and tall stature attract the eye of many, but it is her listening skills and business judgment that attract the dollars. The strongest performing division of the four, Harriet's unit sets the margin aspirations for the overall company. Most internal and external observers believe she is the obvious candidate to become the next CEO. Everyone she manages loves her; she is able to balance high expectations with mercy. Harriet is the first to admit her astounding success has required numerous personal sacrifices along the way. She wishes she had married and had children at some point, but she doubts whether such an opportunity still exists for her. The upcoming strategy meeting is a critical one for her to solidify her status as the next CEO; she is focused early this morning on making sure everything goes well for it. Her hand is trembling slightly, given that she stopped ingesting her nightly bottle of wine four evenings ago. She knows she must maintain complete sobriety for the executive meeting, but she desperately craves a small sip of the single malt whiskey that has so often gotten her through difficult days.

Thus, while the company is conducting an important meeting to trigger new discussions about the direction of the company, the meeting has also triggered a series of uncomfortable emotional cascades among its leaders. The success of Hypothetical Inc. is not entirely dependent on Helen, Horace, Hugo, and Harriet, but the company's success is shaped by their input about the broader emotional dynamic of the company.

Show and Hide

Where there are people, there are emotions. Some of those emotions are expressed openly so that they become part of the group glue, but others are kept locked within individuals. Humans feel together, but each of us also has a private experience not instantly shared or transparent to others.

The long-term decline of community psychosocial support structures (e.g., bowling leagues, churches, barbershop quartets, volunteer groups) has forced individuals to be more alone when they *enter* the workplace. Leaders and frontline associates possess less connectedness to others, even if online networking suggests they have thousands of "friends." Employees at all levels of the hierarchy may also be suffering from a variety of the medical conditions associated with emotional isolation—anxiety, depression, eating disorders, or addictions—even if they seem completely normal to their coworkers. These individual emotional afflictions, in turn, may have serious consequences on the ability of the company as a whole to adapt and perform in the ways necessary for long-term success.

There are emotions we show and others we hide. In modern business life, the reflex is to show very little and to appear impervious. Yet, the reality is that the emotional actions of others can hurt us. Despite their professional success, the four fictional characters each feel a sense of vulnerability in their current circumstance. Every human has to discover how to deal with that vulnerability.

Sources of Individual Emotional Vulnerability

Real-life corporate leaders and entrepreneurs do not simply compute intellectual comparisons with regard to the company; there is a *personal* stake that enters into their perceptions and judgments. What a particular issue means for the business versus what it means for the individual are two entirely different topics, but the emotional impact of one often spills over into the other.

Vulnerability implies neither undesirable weakness nor gentle approachability. In this context, the term denotes the span of all internal physiological and emotional responses to threat.

The same instigators of group conflict first mentioned in Chapter Five (items, ideals, and identity) also are the triggers of individual vulnerability. The universal human desire for safety/security extends not only to our physical body but also to the resources, possessions, values, faiths, freedoms, powers, relationships, and concepts of self to which we anchor ourselves in a world of uncertain risks.

Items, which include tangible objects of value, are reflexively protected from an early age. Toddlers who are attached to a particular toy will resist mightily any attempt to take the toy away (it seems like they learn to say "mine" well before "please" or "thank you"). Adolescents learn to desire material objects, such as smartphones and clothes, as symbols of status in addition to whatever intrinsic value they carry. Adults are deeply possessive of their cars, computers, condos, and other acquisitions. Within the business environment, leaders are naturally protective of their budgets and other department resources. Regardless of the emotional strategy deployed at the broader company level, department leaders will not easily offer resources to other departments (e.g., fictional Horace is anxious about budget cuts). Items possess power.

Ideals are principles or philosophies that provide overarching codes of conduct but also form the basis of vulnerability. The mission, values, ethos, and beliefs dictate people's behaviors but also open people to vulnerabilities. For example, fictional Helen feels saddened and personally threatened by the shift to less nurturance in the company. Fictional Hugo worries about stagnation and eventual failure unless the company redefines itself to match modern circumstances. Ideals can also impact interactions among colleagues in terms of expectations for politeness, respect, autonomy, listening, patience, or forthrightness. Individuals who fail in these respects cause disappointment. When challenges or shifts emerge about the *why* and *how* certain things are done (i.e., objectives, business model, emotional strategy), individuals may become vulnerable and act defensively. They may express this vulnerability openly at the group level or keep it hidden.

Identity is the aggregation of self-perceptions. While every human is a mix of contradictions and inconsistencies, we seek broad labels that define how we face the important challenges of life. Heroic, resilient, beloved, compassionate, brave, and resourceful are ultimately preferable accolades for most people to the alternates. Some other labels (genius, saint, youthful) are atypical in business but equally significant for some people. When business circumstances threaten to remove these labels from us (e.g., will fictional Harriet still be the presumptive CEO after the meeting?), our personal vulnerabilities are heightened. Individuals who lash out after feeling disrespected are demonstrating extreme vulnerability related to their identity. Identity typically also encompasses relational roles, such as spouse, parent, boss, teammate, and friend; if changing business circumstances (or changes in wealth) potentially threaten whom one is married to or friends with, then another layer of emotional vulnerability emerges.

Vulnerabilities define what an individual person idiosyncratically considers important; another person faced with the same crisis will experience different concerns based on different priorities. A change in his or her business circumstances might trigger three nonwork emotional vulnerabilities of items, ideals, and identity simultaneously. If a longtime business leader hears that he may be terminated from a company, his resulting feelings of vulnerability might be from fears of losing his expensive house (item), losing the ability to make large donations to the local children's charity (ideal), or losing his elite recognition in his suburban community (identity).

While some high-minded individuals and spiritual teachings might suggest that the path to spiritual enlightenment is to remove emotional attachments to any of the three categories, the reality is that humans place their intense emotional investment in things that make them feel useful and successful.

Humans have four categories ("boxes") of individual responses to the stress of vulnerability:

1. Positive mental (as demonstrated by fictional Helen)
2. Negative mental (Horace)
3. Positive physical (Hugo)
4. Negative physical (Harriet)

While it is tempting to be judgmental about two of the response boxes, none of these are character types are not fixed. *All of us spend time visiting each box at some point in our lives, depending on the circumstances.* The proportion of time spent in each box likely varies across ages, cultures, demographic parameters, and individual experiences.

Box 1: Positive Mental

Helen represents box 1. As she encounters vulnerability and stress, she is relying on the brain's natural inclinations of connectedness and problem solving to overcome her difficulties. She speaks with her husband, she gathers with her team, she charts progress, and she relies on humor.

The intent of these behaviors is to *shift the brain's focus away from threats* by deeply engaging in something that brings intrinsic satisfaction to the individual. They are brain/mind focused and are positive in their ability to reduce the internal neurotoxicity of vulnerability (i.e., brain-soothing actions).

Social support (i.e., group neurochemistry) is a universal coping mechanism to deal with emotional threats. We feel better after attending a dinner party, taking a friend out for a night on the town, or laughing together at a ridiculous movie.

Hobbies that require concentration, memory, or hand-eye coordination can reduce feelings of stress and vulnerability. These include painting, drawing, pottery, jigsaw puzzles, woodworking, sailing, reading, sewing, collecting stamps/coins, and antique shopping.

Accomplishment in any activity promotes a greater sense of contentment. People who keep checklists for weekend household chores enjoy the pleasure that comes from crossing something off the list when it's done.

Creativity in any form tends to soothe the anxious brain. Children automatically engage in play for this reason, building forts out of cardboard. Even rhythmic scribbling or doodling brings a sense of stability and calmness through creative pattern creation.

Humor, particularly if it triggers the large physical response of laughter, makes anxieties less overwhelming.

Intellectual problem solving, such as the skills used in finishing crossword puzzles or number games in the newspaper, has the great effect of helping to generate positive views of one's own capabilities and persistence.

Voiceless contemplation (also called meditation) is a powerful technique to reduce individual perceptions of vulnerability. Eliminating speech and allowing sensory input to become the full focus of one's attention allows the brain to calm itself by focusing on the external. This can be done during a quiet walk, looking out the window during a rainstorm, sitting in front of a fire, or listening to recordings of chanting monks. The time allows for reframing of concerns and providing self-affirmation. Persons of faith find time for contemplation and prayer to bring spiritual solace.

Mindfulness practices train the brain to recognize signals of the surrounding environment while simultaneously calming internal disruptions.

Box 2: Negative Mental

Horace represents box 2. He micromanages, constantly worries, and looks to escape through online gaming.

In response to feelings of vulnerability, an individual may be prone to fight-flight-freeze reactions of the mind. These negative mental approaches tend to create additional layers of problems rather than allowing the brain to restore itself and address actual problems. *Mental fight responses* attempt to deal with vulnerability by controlling others or lashing out at others. The internal sense of weakness is overcompensated for by external artificial demonstrations of pretend strength. *Mental flight responses* attempt to deal with vulnerability by running away to other imaginary locations or dream worlds. The bad situation of reality is provoking the pain of vulnerability, which the imaginary situation is free of. *Mental freeze responses* attempt to deal with vulnerability by simply waiting for threats to go away or ignoring their existence. This category also includes responses based on attaching helplessness to the vulnerability.

Box 2 coping mechanisms do not reflect reality; these coping mechanisms generate an imaginary milieu that is easier to contend with than reality. While *none of these responses is healthy or appropriate within the workplace*, their presence is common. The goal of a company's emotional strategy should be to prevent or reduce their frequency and pervasiveness.

Micromanagement, overengineering, or becoming a "control freak" are mental responses to feelings of individual vulnerability. Lack of ability to regulate internal feelings leads one to excessively regulate others' behaviors. Some managers are fine during normal work periods but become micromanagers during periods of acute stress/vulnerability.

Bullying represents a mental fight response. Humiliation and hurtful humor have their roots in childhood bullying in schools but are often demonstrated in professional workplaces by immature workers unable to cope with their individual vulnerability.

Elitism is an attack on others. Creation of cliques and pecking order allows the vulnerable individual to feel protected; demeaning others allows the vulnerable individual to feel superior.

Vengeance has the power to consume and obliterate ethical and moral reasoning within a vulnerable individual. If an individual has been wounded in the past (e.g., embarrassed, excluded) during a business situation, his or her response may be to wound others in the company as retribution. This individual response can have the tendency to contagiously spread through groups and cause UPT among stakeholders.

Escapism allows the vulnerable individual to feel safe within an imaginary world of romance, magic, political espionage, or science fiction. Of course, in moderation, dressing up or imagining an alternate life is fine (even healthy). Weekend romps as an alien or a witch can be a terrific stress release. Yet, there is a line that separates reality from fantasy; when it is not clear where the line is, the real problems of a vulnerable individual's life go unaddressed and have implications for loved ones and business colleagues.

Gaming links escapism with physical activity, making it twice as powerful in reducing stress. Within moderation it is a healthy outlet. When an individual lies to play games rather than meet professional or social responsibilities, it has become self-destructive.

Procrastination allows the individual to postpone dealing with the threat until he or she is "ready." The inherent risk of procrastination comes from the potential for threats to grow over time.

Victimization belief freezes the individual. He does not address threats because he believes he deserves it. Guilt overwhelms him for complex reasons. He allows his own anxieties to fester, and he never seeks help. Eventually the sustained neurotoxic effects of vulnerability drive him to exhausted apathy.

Box 3: Positive Physical

Hugo represents box 3. He deals with his stress and emotional vulnerability by providing stimulation to his body rather than his mind. He uses yoga, aromatherapy, and warm baths.

The linkage between mind and body is not a new concept. Ancient philosophers from China, India, and North America embraced techniques to bring together healing from one end of the nervous system (touch, smell, sounds, sight, and taste) to the other (thought and emotion). Many of these concepts have been repackaged for modern marketing but are essentially time-tested wisdom.

The modern medical prevention doctrines of *healthy eating, exercise,* and *sufficient sleep* provide benefits beyond the organs of the abdomen and thorax; they support the function of the brain as well. A healthy body supports not only a healthy mind, but healthy emotion as well. Threats and individual emotional vulnerability may overwhelm a susceptible body that is in poor overall condition.

There are many approaches to cope with individual emotional vulnerability through focus on the physical body. Some of these modalities have rigorous clinical evidence to support their effectiveness, while others simply represent pleasant diversions engaged by those who find them fun.

Exercise that keeps the cardiac muscle and blood vessels in optimal condition allows adequate flow to the brain in times of emotional stress, when vessels tend to clamp down. In the context of managing the physical components of stress, exercise can include weight training, aerobics, sports, rock climbing, walking, cycling, swimming, and all other forms of movement. Of course, such efforts should be done only after consultation with a health-care professional.

Physical excitement (e.g., skiing, skateboarding, riding a roller coaster) is another popular way of coping with stressful circumstances. Assuming that all appropriate safety precautions are followed, these activities can be fun. Some individuals find these activities stressful, however, and should avoid them.

Yoga, tai chi, and *deep breathing* have become enormously popular in the West. They combine many of the box I mental elements with physical movements to reduce stress from vulnerability.

Aromatherapy works based on the concept that the brain areas for smell (olfactory neurons) are adjacent to the areas for emotional and memory processing (amygdala and hippocampus). More than just having fruity smells around, aromatherapy is the systematic use of essential oils to launch multiple neurochemical reactions. The aromas may also be used as a supplement to voiceless contemplation (see box 1).

Self-soothing behaviors include swaying, toe tapping, and other rhythmic repetitive movements. Rocking is especially powerful for emotionally soothing a crying infant. Adults can invoke such rhythmic patterns on their own in stressful moments to calm themselves.

Physical pleasure from chocolate, massage, or a warm bath all may generate emotional peace. Dopamine and serotonin underlie the physical response but also have impacts on the emotional brain areas. In moderation, such treats can be a useful way of counteracting the neurotoxic effects of individual vulnerability.

Singing and *dancing* are fun ways to clear emotional toxins out of the system. These are activities that can be done in the privacy of one's home without an audience; no panel of three judges is required in order to have fun crooning along to MP3 favorites in pajamas. Intrinsic joy from the acts of singing and dancing partly explains why musical behaviors have been preserved for millennia of human existence across many cultures and languages.

Box 4: Negative Physical

Harriet represents box 4. She is suffering from addiction.

It may be judgmentally tempting to view this box as the cage for undesirable unprofessional individuals, but *everyone will find themselves in this box at some point in their lives*: saint and sinner, entry level and executive, righteous and ruthless. Everyone experiences moments where the only perceived outlet to the accumulating effects of stress is to alter our bodies through actions that may be hurtful to others.

To repeat the message from box 2, while *none of these responses is healthy or appropriate within the workplace*, their presence is common. The goal of a company's emotional strategy is to reduce their frequency and pervasiveness.

Alcohol addiction appears in many obvious as well as less obvious forms. There are weekend binge drinkers, inconsistent work performers (who are never seen drinking but miss document deadlines), and perfect workers who hide their addictions, like Harriet. Employee assistance programs are a needed remedy to support many colleagues struggling with this mental illness.

Drug addiction includes traditional well-publicized items, such as cocaine and prescription sedatives, but may also involve substances available in industrial workplaces, such as inhaled solvents.

Behavioral compulsions/addictions include a broad range of activities, such as gambling, shopping, Internet surfing, and risk taking ("thrill junkies"). These may be more difficult to detect but can have equally disastrous consequences for an enterprise, particularly if company funds are used for gambling or excessive risk taking.

Sex can become an inappropriate means of coping with office stress. Rather than a normal part of human experience between consenting individuals, preoccupation with sex can create numerous business problems. Casting aside moral judgments, extramarital affairs with colleagues are not harmless if they impair the ability of team members to collaborate. The corporate executive who rapidly depletes his considerable income in strip clubs (in part driven by the adrenaline-backed thrill of the forbidden) may become desensitized to risk taking in important strategic decisions for the company. Preoccupation with sex may also promote unwanted advances toward coworkers, which has the business implication of sexual harassment lawsuits.

Food as a coping mechanism can manifest as undereating or overeating. Some executives will exhibit bulimic behavioral patterns to maintain a particular appearance. Some of this particular reaction to threat/vulnerability comes from the specifics of the hormones (e.g., cortisol) that impact blood sugar biochemistry.

Violence in the workplace makes headlines but is fortunately a rare exception. Nonetheless, it does represent a potential reaction to vulnerability/threat.

* * *

How Now

- *Understand individual vulnerability as a threat to corporate success.* Businesses are comprised of humans; thus, businesses are vulnerable. Self-destruction happens to individuals and potentially to businesses as a result. Businesses must therefore protect themselves by utilizing emotional strategies (Chapter Six) that support connectedness and enable individuals to cope with their stresses.

- *Have an organizational psychologist or counselor regularly available to staff.* Leaders generally have little awareness of the stress their employees experience. Have a counselor come once a month or twice per quarter to speak to people anonymously in one-on-one sessions.

- *Support intense periods with counselors.* Intense work generates intense emotions. If an organization is exceptionally stressed (as described in Chapter Seven) or has a major turnaround effort going on, then counselors on-site can be effective in helping employees deal with the vulnerability of the chaos.

- *Understand when you personally enter boxes 2 and 4.* Do a self-assessment to understand when circumstances push you into the negative mental and negative physical responses. Which vulnerabilities (items, ideals, and identity) most often trigger you into a downward spiral? Do you start out sad, angry, or scared when you enter boxes 2 and 4?

- *Listen.* Colleagues under stress do not always keep their anxieties secret. Be on the lookout for subtle cues that someone feels overwhelmed and vulnerable. Then, be prepared to listen (see Chapter Nine).

Chapter Eleven:
The Good News

A movement of creating emotionally successful companies has already begun.

Successful businesses across the world today are already implementing the philosophies, strategies, and tactics described in the previous ten chapters.

Customers are being respected for their troubles, time, and tastes, as well as their transaction.

Team leaders, who intuitively sense when an unexpected handwritten note of appreciation or a moment of silliness is exactly what their team needs to keep pressing toward an ambitious goal, are guiding teammates to greatness.

Dedicated chiefs are advocating for the pressing needs of their colleagues while finding common ground with those with whom they must join forces.

Esteemed organizations have been conducting business for decades (or even centuries) with prioritized attention to the need for employee professional development, collegial cohesiveness, and pushing the limits of imagination as to what their products can do for the world.

Newer companies are generating buzz not only for their products but also for their approach to people.

Millions of employees are discovering that work partnership and friendship can coexist, that artificial separations between business and emotion only inhibit the success people seek in both realms. They are uniting over the quantifiable and the inspirational, with room for both laughter and logic.

Every day in businesses large and small, across every corner of this planet, someone feels overwhelmed and someone else comes to that person's aid to listen to his or her anxieties and pain.

Where did these wondrous connections begin?

Most are not the result of programmatic, structured decisions by senior management. Rather, some of the connections emanate from opportunistic desire, seizing a momentary chance to gain an additional customer by redefining how to engage with them. Or, a disastrous year prompts two business units to seek synergy rather than suspicion. Some of the greatest companies of the past fifty years have simply transmitted the emotional strategy of their founder and leader, even if the term "emotional strategy" has never been voiced before.

So, there is much to be excited about. Many emotionally visionary individuals are out in the world, sponsoring emotional connectedness in ways that allow their businesses to flourish; many examples are already formed to instruct the rest of the business world about how to do things the right emotional way.

But it isn't everywhere, it isn't all the time, and it hasn't improved business conditions for everyone.

Companies continue to fail, not from a lack of market awareness or product flaws but from an inability to fully embrace the role of emotion with their customers, teams, stakeholders, and organizations.

Excitement for what is already happening must inspire legions of others to share in that progress. After all, is a street considered safe if two houses have alarms and the other five have been burglarized? Most companies still have the chance to considerably improve their earnings by striving for emotional excellence.

The list of winners and losers in an emotional economy will continue to grow; both will receive attention. Academics will document the ways in which those who utilize emotions in commerce become successful and drive economic growth. Business school curriculum will include case studies of how ignorance of emotion leads to business tragedy. Observers will come to say of some company implosions, "Oh, of course that venture failed—they never worked out what to do with emotions."

Just as various business leaders have remarked on the need for more mathematics and science graduates to keep pace with the business demands of the future, those same business leaders must call to the kindergartens and colleges alike to educate youth in the emotional collaboration skills necessary for business to flourish in this century.

If one examines the most successful new ventures of the past twenty years in Internet search, airlines, smartphones, coffee, rental cars, social networking, online shoe retailing, and numerous other industries, a distinctive business model has been matched by a distinctive emotional strategy. The superstar companies have outperformed industry competitors, in part because they have embraced the concept of emotional connectedness within their business enterprise.

Imagine if a modern company suggested constructing their headquarters office building *without toilets*. Someone in management might offer a litany of reasons about costs and wasted productivity as a rationale for the policy. Employees would revolt while onlookers would shake their heads in disbelief. Legal activists would eventually offer, "Having a restroom is not a convenience or a nice-to-have benefit. It is a biological necessity arising out of human physiology that must be available in a human workplace." Soon, as knowledge of the emotional nature of the brain becomes more widespread, we'll begin to use the same reasoning for including emotions in the headquarters as for including bathrooms. It's just a workplace necessity arising out of human physiology.

For the company just beginning, emotional strategy can become the foundation for daily operations in a way that people will accept as "the way we work around here." Just as there must be intolerance for reckless spending, there must be intolerance for reckless indifference to colleagues. The first business plan shared with angel investors should not define only the value creation model, but the emotional connectedness model for customers and the team as well.

For the larger established company that is currently struggling due to industry collapse, lack of available lending, or a disenchanted customer base, there is still hope. It will not be easy, but a transformation initiative that encompasses redesign of operations and an emotionally guided marketing plan can serve as a revolutionary road map to reignite performance.

The successful, industry-leading multinational business understands the importance of agility. It takes miles to change the trajectory of an oil tanker, and similarly it will take years to embrace the organizational changes needed to succeed in the currently shifting business climate. *Emotional Business* principles will become a part of recruiting, architecture, orientation, leadership, capability building, performance evaluation, and compensation. To begin, this requires careful deliberations with the board of directors. No future strategic plan will be complete without recognition of emotional strategy. When shareholders accept ubiquitous persistent threat to be the biggest drain on earnings, policies and management approaches that support emotional connectedness will follow.

Leaders and frontline staff will not only improve the success of their businesses by increased skill in the six forms of listening, but may find (as those organizations who have already adopted *Emotional Business* principles have found) that introducing greater emotional sophistication into their business naturally carries over into personal relationships and community presence as well. If you get the emotion right, you get the business right. Change the business, and you change the world.

Imagine if the term "corporate bond" could come to mean both a financial instrument as well as a description of the kindness between coworkers.

At the very beginning of this text, the one-handed civilization parable described the effects of intentional limitation over one-half of human capability. Intentional limitations over human emotional capabilities for the past two hundred years are now coming to an end. Now, the type of work, where we work, and how we work demand a new paradigm based on the emotional tendencies of the species.

We will come to view the term "emotional business" as duplicative. We have the freedom to fashion a two-handed world, where emotion and traditional business fundamentals must not only coexist but thrive together.

Appendix:
All the Lists in One Place

Here are all the lists in one place.

Chapter 1
Drivers of Increasing Need for Emotional Excellence
1. Outputs of business have evolved
2. Role of people vis-à-vis machines has changed
3. Customers are emotionally aware/savvy
4. Emotionally volatile customers

Three Emotional Hurdles of Commerce
1. Is it safe to spend? (trust in systems)
2. Does this item meet my need? (trust in services)
3. Is this the right person/place to buy from? (trust in seller)

Emotional Interfaces in Business
1. Customer
2. Team
3. Oppositional stakeholders
4. Organization

How Now (Setting a Tone)
1. Integrate emotional strategy into business planning.
2. Leaders should give a vision address.

Chapter 2
How Now (Building Emotional Awareness)
1. Companies teach emotional awareness skills.
2. Business schools teach emotional awareness skills.
3. Grandparents and parents teach emotional awareness skills.

Chapter 3
Customer Emotional Experiences
R = Responsiveness: "Troubles"
S = Special status: "Top of the list"
T = Tender loving care (TLC)
U = Uniqueness (customization): "Tastes"
V = Velocity: "Time"
W = Wow factor: "Ta-da!"
X = Extra: "Tons"

Customer Experience as the Basis for Trust
Responsiveness = Protection
Special status = Loyalty
TLC = Friendship/affinity
Uniqueness = Freedom
Velocity = Instant fulfillment
Wow factor = Amazement
Extra = Abundance

Responsive Elements
1. Accessibility
2. Status transparency

Special Status Acknowledgment Tactics
1. Price reductions/rebates only for elite customers
2. Upgrades in products/services only for elite customers, faster process
3. Gifts outside of the core business product/service only for elite customers
4. Written and face-to-face expressions of gratitude only for elite customers
5. Special experiences only for elite customers

Options for a "Wow" Result
1. Unexpectedly strong degree of result achieved
2. Unexpected qualitative nature of result achieved
3. Unexpectedly fun or impressive delivery mechanism
4. Unanticipated ancillary benefits

Options for Demonstrating "Extra"
1. Abundance/tangible volume
2. Absence of deceit/transparent written comparison

How Now (Serving Emotional Needs of Customers)
1. Clarify the company's emotional priorities today, and build an infrastructure to deliver emotion to customers.
2. Executives and managers should observe the retail experience.
3. Ask the customers.

Chapter 4
Objectives of a Team
1. Deliver
2. Decide

Team Cancers
1. Apathy
2. Gossip
3. Hypercompetitiveness
4. Humiliation
5. Defensiveness
6. Sabotage
7. Deflection of accountability
8. Perfectionism
9. Micromanagement from distrust

Speaking Truth to Power
1. Say, "I feel compelled to say something that you may not want to hear." (Pause for one second.)
2. Say, "Your [appearance/behavior/mind-set] makes me [emotional adjective] and is affecting the team." (Pause again.)
3. Ask, "Can we discuss this now or at a later hour?"

How Now (Building and Supporting Emotional Teams)
1. Compose teams based on emotional contributions.
2. Begin with a Team Charter document (and discussion).
3. Track team perceptions with a Team Emotional Barometer.
4. Mandate facilitators for emotional discussion.
5. Prepare a "Plan B" for impending implosion.

Chapters 4 and 6
Team Emotional Needs and Emotional Business Strategies
1. Progress/achievement
2. Peace
3. Nurturance/development
4. Inspiration

5. Inclusion
6. Imagination/excitement of possibility
7. Gratitude
8. Fun
9. Friendship

Chapter 5
Ubiquitous Persistent Threat "Earnings Drainers"
1. Revising, reworking, and redoing value-adding tasks due to avoidance of communicating alignment up front
2. Bureaucratic cover-your-a** (CYA) activities rather than core value-adding functions
3. Delaying internal transfer of data/best practices/customer relationship messaging due to paranoia of what will be done with particular information by other internal groups
4. Inordinate time spent by leaders in negotiations/lobbying for internal resources rather than creating value
5. Sabotaging reputations or performance of other units of the company (especially if KPIs/incentives are based on comparative performance)

Symptom Checklist of Internal Opposition
1. Reinventing the wheel
2. Decisions are not final
3. Machinelike work environment
4. Isolation
5. Secrets
6. No plan B
7. Extinguished enthusiasm
8. Overproduction out of fear
9. Clumsy about conflict

Reducing Business Impact of Opposition
1. Prevention
2. Decoupling UPT from business practices
3. Redefining the paradigm of success for opponents
4. Fix emotional relations/reduce fighting between parties

Decoupling UPT from Business Practices
1. Processing templates to reduce rework
2. Automation of transactional activities that lead to strife
3. Outsourcing selected activities of disproportionate impact

Redefining the Paradigm of Success
1. Grand exchange/give up on outcome A to win outcome B
2. Mosaic of winning pieces
3. Nuclear option/entirely remove the point of conflict

Primitive Responses to Threat
1. Fight
2. Flight
3. Freeze

Fix Emotional Relations with Opponents
1. Forgiveness
2. Flowers
3. Feedback
4. Fun/"fyzical"
5. Friendship
6. Facilitator
7. Focus

How Now (Reducing UPT and Conflicts)
1. Assess the nine distrust symptoms (UPT) in your organization.
2. Get over it. If you have had a long-standing feud with someone in your company, it's time to end it.
3. Push for compromise.

Chapter 6
Progress as Emotional Strategy
1. "Keep things moving"
2. Pride, accomplishment, and sense of achievement
3. Small reminders in hallways of everything accomplished
4. New candidates assessed for achievement orientation.
5. Leadership positions for promoted internal candidates
6. Time management skills
7. Scorecards, visual management, checklists
8. Performance reviews: no surprises, set targets, fix problems

Peace as Emotional Strategy
1. "No UPT zone"
2. Joint sacrifice, respectfulness, knowledge sharing, and adaptability
3. Sense of harmony
4. Keep out the jerks and hotheads
5. Listening skills/diplomacy in initial onboarding program
6. Training is for learning and bridge building
7. Leaders and managers must listen/Clinton-Mandela skills/abrasive employees are terminated
8. Compensation emphasizes fairness plus bonus (company performance)

Nurturance as Emotional Strategy

1. "We take care of customers and each other"
2. Physical nourishment, quiet spaces for rejuvenation
3. Recruit talent willing to be mentored, and mentor others.
4. Building internal talent rather than hiring it from the outside
5. Role modeling and mentoring more than formal training
6. Managers are mentors/coaches who build relationships.
7. Metrics such as "followership"
8. Earnings are reinvested into employee quality of life.

Inspiration as Emotional Strategy

1. "Imagine all we can do"
2. Belief in the greater good/shared involvement in society
3. Photographs/symbols/quotes in hallways
4. Talent assessment includes discussing impact of one's work
5. New employees are noble individuals making a contribution
6. Training and mentoring are road map to future state
7. Managers: "servant leader" model or the eloquent orator
8. Subjective component of 360-degree evaluations/ reward volunteerism

Inclusion as Emotional Strategy

1. "Speak up!"
2. Sense of belonging and respect

3. Rare to find a quiet hallway/flyer boards, large group spaces
4. Corporate recognition of frontline worker ideas
5. Recruit talent comfortable with considering multiple points of view.
6. The only "sin" is withholding a great idea or serious warning. Mocking another person's idea is unacceptable.
7. Decisions take time. Leaders listen in different forms.
8. Everyone gets at least one chance to shine and be the hero.
9. Willingness to uphold "obligation to dissent"
10. Avoid disproportionate bonus structures.

Imagination as Emotional Strategy

1. Big ideas generate big emotion!
2. Bonding through contributing small pieces to a big answer.
3. Recruit individuals comfortable with running with an idea.
4. Employees must find intrinsic pleasure at solving problems.
5. Leaders keep people joyous about doing the impossible.
6. Evaluation emphasizes intellectual contributions.
7. Compensation includes big bonuses/rewarding revolution

Gratitude as Emotional Strategy

1. "To whom do I owe my success?"
2. Gathering to reflect/thank as a means of creating unity
3. Visual recognition of legacy in hallways/ thank-you notes

4. Recruit talent who embody "emotional sales relationships."
5. Daily operations include civility (please/thank you).
6. Mix of verbal, written, gifts, and recognition to employees
7. Avoid unfair bonuses that make some feel undervalued.

Fun as Emotional Strategy
1. "Don't be the party pooper."
2. Fun can be the antidote to UPT.
3. Bright colors, toys, photos, action figure dolls, artwork
4. Onboarding reshapes attitudes about the nature of work.
5. Necessary to have people depart early if it is a poor fit
6. Learning must be linked with playing; avoid long lectures.
7. Leaders set targets and then get out of the way for joy to lead.
8. Measurement emphasizes customer service and colleagues.
9. Fun cannot be a trick to avoid paying people decent wages.

Friendship as Emotional Strategy
1. "No friendless islands"
2. Seamless contract implies friends in work and life
3. Recruiting has to discuss social expectations up front.
4. "Social cultivation" for top talent outside of the office
5. Orientation includes large name tags and icebreakers.

6. Training programs include time for socializing.
7. Leaders must be aware of the withdrawn or disengaged.
8. Abrasive individuals must receive corrective guidance.
9. Avoid unfair or disproportionate compensation.

Mistakes in Implementing Emotional Strategy
1. Starting strong and then fading
2. Trying to keep everyone happy
3. Doing the superficial but not the serious
4. Being inconsistent

How Now (Embedding Emotional Strategy)
1. The board of directors should expect an emotional strategy summary from the CEO.
2. Investors and analysts should expect an emotional strategy summary from an entrepreneur or company.
3. Leaders integrate an emotional strategy component into existing strategic planning.
4. Select managers carefully.

Chapter 7
Descent to Emotional Destruction
1. Disconnected/absent emotional strategy
2. Disruptive event occurs (minor or major)
3. Entrance of behavioral "F responses"
4. Greed and punishment strategies enhanced
5. Emotional destruction ends in business failure

Emotional Resuscitation Program
1. Bold announcement/acknowledge what went wrong

2. Temporary shutdown to recover; engage counselors; listen
3. Definition of new emotional strategy
4. Implementation of new strategy
5. Follow-up discussions to ensure chosen strategy is working

How Now (Ameliorating Toxic Environments)
1. Be better at decisions.
2. Change things from the ground up through training, forming networks, providing feedback to each other.
3. Use data/estimate financial costs of bad environment.
4. Reduce unfair surprises and broken promises.

Decision-Making Roles
1. Trigger: "Let's end discussion and vote."
2. Menu: "Have we identified all the options?"
3. Facts: "Let's run the numbers and get the data."
4. Implications: "What are the risks? Do we have a plan B?"
5. Mechanism: "Is this a vote or consensus?"

Chapter 8
Changing the Oil
1. Thinking events
2. Enjoyment events
3. Act-for-change events
4. Reflection/gratitude events

Verbal Formats to Create Alignment
1. Numbers
2. Logical arguments
3. Future state vision/outcome
4. Promises

5. Myth/story/example
6. Humor
7. Empathy

How Now (Leaders Impact Group Neurochemistry)
1. Schedule a gathering to change the oil.
2. Adapt internal communications to include all seven language formats.
3. Adapt external communications to include all seven language formats.
4. Manage upward using all seven formats.

Chapter 9
Forms of Listening
1. Release of anger
2. Fast fulfillment of a need
3. Affirmation in periods of uncertainty/fear
4. Problem-solving support
5. Shared joy
6. Supportive nurturance during pain

Listening to Anger
1. "HVAC": heating, ventilation, air-conditioning.
2. Let them keep going until the fire burns itself out.
3. Listener stillness brings calmness to the situation.
4. Don't ever interrupt an angry individual.
5. Pause, and then acknowledge their pain, disappointment, etc.

Listening to Urgency
1. Recognize action need (product/service correction) and emotional need for resolution.
2. Speakers do not feel secure, so give them security.
3. "We'll make this right." Then solve the problem.
4. Verbalize "resolution before regret."

Listening to Uncertainty/Fear

1. Speakers need space to unload their thoughts and hopes.
2. Be open and be nonjudgmental.
3. Use undivided attention/"focused laser" approach.
4. Fairly little needs to be said at first; let them get it out.
5. Provide simple affirmations.

Listening to Support Problem Solving

1. When confused, "talk it out" with a receptive listener.
2. Avoid giving advice directly until asked.
3. This is a dance that the speaker leads.
4. The best response to everything is another question.

Listening to Share Joy

1. Humans feel joy together.
2. Let happy people have their moment.
3. This is a happy dance. Match them in the dance.
4. Nonverbal signals are a higher priority than spoken words.
5. Offer congratulations or expressions of significance.
6. Offer statements of emotional data.
7. Avoid analysis.

Listening to Support through Pain

1. Providing support through devastating emotional shocks (grief, betrayal, resentment).
2. Allow speakers to fully release whatever anguish they have.
3. Apply firm pressure on forearm or shoulder (only if speaker is comfortable with contact).

4. Be expressive, sympathetic, and reassuring.
5. Avoid "I know how you feel."
6. Avoid "Don't be so sensitive."

Clinton-Mandela Skills
1. Eye contact
2. Smiling
3. Slowed cadence
4. Inflections of voice volume
5. Touch

How Now (Listening)
1. Train executives in listening. Leaders have two reasons to listen: absorb key ideas from others, and shift group neurochemistry through connectedness.
2. Train frontline associates in listening. This will help reduce frustrations within the company as well as improve interactions with customers.
3. Practice listening and Clinton-Mandela skills everywhere. With the spouse, children, friends, the mailman, etc.

Chapter 10
Sources of Individual Vulnerability
1. Items
2. Ideals
3. Identity

Box 1: Positive Mental
1. Social interaction
2. Hobbies
3. Achievement and accomplishment
4. Creativity/doodling
5. Humor/laughter

6. Intellectual problem solving, puzzles, or number games
7. Voiceless contemplation/observation; for persons of faith, prayer and self-reflection
8. Mindfulness practices

Box 2: Negative Mental
1. Micromanagement/overengineering/"control freak"
2. Verbal abuse
3. Elitism and hierarchical subjugation/creating cliques
4. Vengeance/preoccupation of hurting others as retribution
5. Escapism
6. Procrastination/avoidance
7. Victimization mind-set (via guilt)

Box 3: Positive Physical
1. Healthy eating and sufficient sleep
2. Exercise (weight training, aerobics, sports, rock climbing, walking, cycling, swimming, and all forms of movement)
3. Physical excitement derived from movement
4. Yoga, tai chi, and forms of deep breathing
5. Aromatherapy
6. Self-soothing behaviors, rhythmic movement
7. Chocolate, massage, and warm baths
8. Singing and dancing

Box 4: Negative Physical
1. Alcohol addiction
2. Drug addiction
3. Behavioral addiction (gambling, risk taking, shopping)
4. Preoccupation with sex
5. Food (undereating, overeating)
6. Violence

How Now (Vulnerability, Stress, and Coping)
1. Understand individual vulnerability as a threat to corporate success. Self-destruction happens to individuals and potentially to businesses as a result.
2. Have an organizational psychologist or counselor regularly available to staff.
3. Support intense periods with counselors.
4. Understand when you personally enter boxes 2 and 4.
5. Listen. Be on the lookout for subtle cues that someone feels overwhelmed and vulnerable.

About the Author

Dr. Ravi Rao assists organizations and startups to improve culture, strategic alignment, operational efficiency, and leadership practices through focusing on traditional business fundamentals in addition to organizational emotion. He is a keynote speaker at numerous conferences, including the Society of Emotional Intelligence. Before becoming a management consultant to multinational companies and international charities, Dr. Rao was a child health researcher and a neurosurgeon-in-training at Harvard's Children's Hospital of Boston. He is a graduate of Johns Hopkins University and the University of Virginia. He lives in Chicago. *Emotional Business* is his first book.

Additional Reading

Dr. Ravi Rao highly recommends the following books for diverse perspectives on infant brain development, emotion, and business organizations:

Sarah Blaffer Hrdy (2011). *Mothers and Others: The Evolutionary Origins of Mutual Understanding*. Belknap Press.

Louis Cozolino (2006). *The Neuroscience of Human Relationships: Attachment and the Developing Social Brain*. Norton & Company.

Daniel Goleman (2006). *Emotional Intelligence: Why It Can Matter More Than IQ, 10th Anniversary Edition*. Bantam.

Marco Iacoboni (2008). *Mirroring People: The Science of Empathy and How We Connect with Others*. Farrar, Straus & Giroux.

Thomas Lewis, Fari Amini & Richard Lannon (2000). *A General Theory of Love*. Random House.

Robert Sutton (2007). *The No Asshole Rule: Building a Civilized Workplace and Surviving One That Isn't*. Business Plus.

Contacting Dr. Ravi Rao

Dr. Ravi Rao maintains a website with an active mailing list, offering new thoughts on current events and invitations to his public seminars. He welcomes making new connections.

He also speaks *pro bono* to congregations and faith-based organizations.

Visit **www.emotionalbusinesssuccess.com** for more details and to join the mailing list.

CPSIA information can be obtained at www.ICGtesting.com
Printed in the USA
BVOW071834300812

299113BV00002B/136/P

9 781475 926187